Barefoot in Siargao

Nature • Adventure • Ghost
Stories from Siargao Island

Written and Illustrated by

Christina Camingue Buo

Featuring the art of Portrait Artist MANUEL PAÑARES

D1492775

ISBN
978-1-5437-4279-4 (sc)
978-1-5437-4278-7 (e)

Library of Congress Control Number: 2022909379

Print information available on the last page.

To order additional copies of this book, contact
Toll Free 800 101 2657 (Singapore)
Toll Free 1 800 81 7340 (Malaysia)
www.partridgepublishing.com/singapore
orders.singapore@partridgepublishing.com

05/31/2018

PARTRIDGE

To my grandparents -

Josefina Diaz Navarro

Whose strong mind, generous spirit and loving heart inspired not only one man and one family, but also an entire community;

Dr. Pedro Gonzaga Camingue

A true gentleman who exemplified honest, humble and selfless service as the first medical doctor of Siargao Island

And my grand-uncle –

Antonio Gonzaga Camingue

Former mayor of General Luna and Chairman of the Mayors League of Surigao (1938-1940), he initiated reforms and fought for the independence of Barrio Cabuntog, a leading copra producer, from the town of Dapa, which led to the creation of the municipality of General Luna (in 1929) which he named after his idolized revolutionary hero, Gen. Antonio Luna; he helped found the Liberal Political Party in Siargao and supported the cause of education; a visionary, patriotic and courageous leader, he dedicated his life in faithful service to the community.

Acknowledgements

The author and publisher gratefully acknowledge the following publications where some stories in this book have previously appeared in a different version. These stories have been entirely rewritten for inclusion in this collection.

The Freeman Sunday Magazine: "A Girl Named Lucita" (6 October 1996)

Sun.Star Weekend: "The Dance of the Firefly" (13 February 2000)

Cebu Daily News: "Birds in the Wild" (8 December 2012)

"Surigao Rising" (4 October 2008)

"Spellbinding Sohoton" (15 April 2000)

Siargao Island News Magazine: "Song for the Birds" (March 2014)

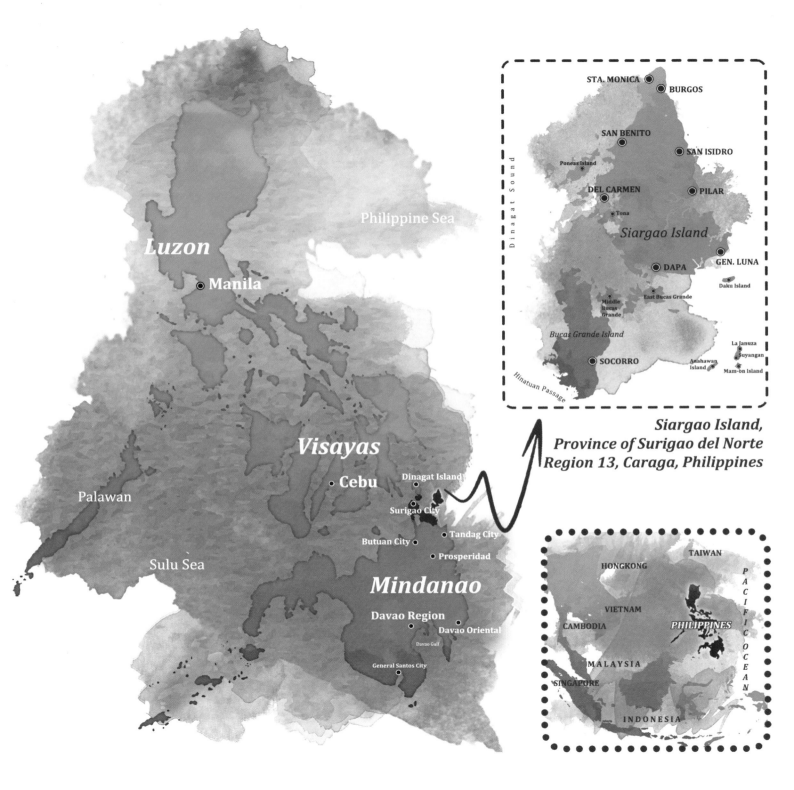

Siargao Island,
Province of Surigao del Norte
Region 13, Caraga, Philippines

Contents

The boys saw something that floated – a lady in white with long, black hair, visible in the silvery moonlight.

THE
White Lady
AND THE
Tambis Tree

Among my fondest childhood memories are those summers I spent in the home of my maternal grandparents in the town of General Luna in Siargao Island, where my grandfather, Pedro Gonzaga Camingue, served as the first (charity) doctor. He was the first to open a medical practice in Siargao in the late 1930s, serving in many rural villages and remote towns until he retired in the 1980s. The summer holidays in Siargao became a yearly family excursion. Our home was in Cebu City, where my father, Jose, worked in a bank, and my mother, Evelyn, was employed with the Regional Trial Court (Branch 16), but it was my mom who insisted on taking us to the island every summer, where we spent our days roaming the countryside, running about the beach and swimming in the jellyfish-studded lagoon. It was our best summer place, the sanctuary of our hopes and dreams and the paradise of our childhood.

There were picnics on the beach and in the farm, hopping from Guyam Island to Daku, and wonderful parties. Our grandparents, parents, aunts, and uncles never spoon-fed us; we, the young fry, were left to our own devices and played outdoors with abandon, climbing up grandmother's *tambis*[1] tree, storytelling and playing imaginative games in the tree house in the *plaza*[2], learning how to ride a bike around the kiosk with our cousins, Tomelyn, Ken, Dahlyn, Sherlyn, Ian-maro and their brothers and sisters; racing along the beachfront school grounds with *amor seco*[3] sticking to our clothes, running free in the woods, reveling in the cool summer rain, swinging on a tire suspended from a crooked coconut palm trunk on a secluded beach, hunting for *kayabang* or beach crabs when the moon was full, lying back on the sand and counting stars falling from the night sky and dancing on the beach in the moonlight. But the best thing about our summer vacation was the boundless hospitality of my maternal grandparents. *Lola*[4] Deding and *Lolo* Indong loved people with real, generous affection. They welcomed everybody into their home. I remember the front door of the house stood always open. It was filled with all kinds of people from all walks of life. It rang with voices and laughter day after day. A steady stream of visitors from the church, rural health unit, government offices, farmers and fisher folk, family, relatives, friends, children, and grandchildren came and went. When I think of summer, I think of *Lola* and *Lolo* and our ancestral home in Siargao Island.

Summer 1985.

The house was bustling with domestic activity at five o'clock in the afternoon. In the *pantaw*[5], the helpers were busy lighting several Petromax lamps; some were husking early maturing rice or *pilipig* using wooden mortar and pestle (*lusong ug ayho*) while others were winnowing rice or *humay* in a flat basket or *nigo*. *Lola Deding*, a small and slender woman with short, wavy hair and wearing a green print duster, came out of the *tindahan* or store through the back door, and made her way across the store room up the long flight of stairs, that led to the kitchen, which smelt mouth-wateringly of delicious cooking. She ran the household with a big retinue of domestic helpers, most of them working students whom she supported throughout their elementary and high school years. She has been on her feet since sunup overseeing the general merchandise store on the ground floor and now she was in the *kusina* or kitchen, supervising the preparation and cooking of an elaborate dinner for her children and grandchildren who were vacationing from Cebu and Surigao.

Ancestral Home, Christina Buo, 2015.

My maternal grandparents welcomed everybody into their home and my doctor-grandfather could have graced the top rank of a major hospital in the city but he refused the offer and stayed in the island to be of service to the people, providing medical services where none existed before.

The fragrant *tagnijogan na kayabang*[6] simmered in fresh coconut milk; *tinuya na Bayo* soup with *tangyad*[7] steamed in a saucepan; *Manok Bisaya* or native chicken began to sizzle in the pan; *pinaksiw na buntog* and *heringero*[8] stewed in coconut vinegar and garlic; golden brown calamari served hot and crispy on China dishes and plates; *kalabasa* pies made straight from pumpkins freshly picked from the farm. On the kitchen counter were a big bowl of shark fin soup and a platter of *bangsi na buwad* or salted and sun-dried flying fish, ready to be served with steamed white rice.

"Anita, could you help me peel the *camote?*" said Lina, the long-time household cook who was carrying a large iron pot of steaming sweet potato to the dirty kitchen.

"Be right there," answered Anita, who was seated on the kitchen table, snacking on boiled *Carnaba*[9] while pouring a big bottle of *ginamos na poot-poot*, a traditional salted fish paste, on to small China plates. Almost everybody in the family has a craving for this appetizer. *Poot-poot,* which belongs to the Sardines family, is found and caught in the *butohanan* or the Pisangan Reef, the town's natural coral barrier from the powerful waves of the Pacific Ocean.

At a quarter past five, *Lola* Deding leaned over and flicked the talk button on the intercom mounted on a wooden post, next to the *Frigidaire*[10] , "Percy, tell the kids to come up now for the Angelus."

"Yes, *Tia*[11]," replied Percy, who was trusted to make everything work smoothly in the general merchandise store on the ground floor.

Soon the voices of more than a dozen children shouting could be heard as they ran up the main stairway, then faded to a whisper as soon as they joined the whole family kneeling at the altar of the living room, saying the six o'clock Angelus Prayer.

The Angel of the Lord declared to Mary:
And she conceived of the Holy Spirit.
Hail Mary...

Behold the handmaid of the Lord:
Be it done to me according to your word.
Hail Mary...

And the Word was made flesh:
And dwelt among us
Hail Mary...

Pray for us, O Holy Mother of God.
That we may be made worthy of the promises of Christ

Let Us Pray:
Pour forth we beseech You, O Lord, Your grace into our hearts that we, to whom the incarnation of Christ, Your Son, was made known by the message of an angel, may by His passion and cross be brought to the glory of His resurrection, through the same Christ our Lord, Amen.

In the gathering dusk, the large house with wood-framed sliding glass windows or *bintana*, is aglow with Petromax lamps and there, laid out on the dining tables, was a sumptuous feast. Dinner proceeded gaily afterward. We, children, ate in the small dining area right next to the kitchen while *Lolo* and *Lola*, our mother, father, uncles, and aunts feasted in the main dining hall.

Afterward, we gathered around *Lola* in the *jamoyaon*[12] rectangular dining table as she made an accounting of the day's sales. She was well over sixty but she had excellent vision; she wore no eye glasses. *Lolo,* who listened more than he talked, would retire to his favorite wooden rocking chair by the large window in the *sala*[13] and listen or sing along to his favorite Visayan love songs, *Usahay* and *Matud Nila*, playing on his turntable phonograph record player. Sometimes he would request all of us, his grandchildren or *apo*, to dance for him.

My Dapa-born grandmother, Josefina "Deding", was a legendary beauty in her time. She raised and reared eight children, operated a pioneering transport business and set up one of the first general stores in town.

The best thing about our summer vacation in Siargao Island was the loving care and generosity of our grandparents, Pedro and Josefina.

As children, we loved to play with our reflection in the mirror and after dinner, we sat at the main table and made monkey faces in the mirror-like finish of the Petromax lamp base. My brother, Josephus, nicknamed Tottie, raised his eyebrows and flared his nostrils like a *kabaw* or water buffalo, while my cousin, Ian, glared at himself and stuck out his tongue, which had all of us laughing wildly. We made a hilarious expression on our faces, contorting and twisting them hard to look like aliens from outer space.

Suddenly, there was a sound of hands clapping outside the street. For us, it was a sign and an invitation to join our cousins and friends for an evening gambol.

"That's Lyndon calling," said my cousin, Roy, to his brothers.

"We better go. We've got plans tonight."

About half past eleven o'clock, the boys gathered in a dark corner off the main street, outside the house of Mauricio Gonzaga Ravelo. *Lolo* Ores, as we called him, was the Mayor of the Municipality of General Luna for two consecutive terms, 1964-1967 and 1967-1971. He and his wife had a garden with a *tambis* tree in it. It was walled in from the street. It is now fully grown and in the summer months, the *tambis* ripens and bears pink, sweet, juicy, fruits with smooth pink skin. On this day in May, the tree is heavily laden with clusters of bell-shaped, shiny pink *tambis*, something to tempt the boys.

We, girls, were curled up in a corner, under the lamp post, about ten meters away, listening to our neighbors, Arlene (Baby), Anita (Deh-deh) and Annie tell blood-curdling tales of *ayok*[14], *sigbin*[15], *duwende*[16], *santelmo*[17] and tobacco-smoking *kapre*[18]. The night is warm and hushed and the moon shone out between the clouds.

"Now Andy," his elder brother, Roy, began in a whisper, "you'll stay out here and be our watchman. Take this flashlight and give us a sign if you see someone coming!"

The boys climbed over the wall, tiptoed through the dark garden and were up in the *tambis* tree quicker than a wink. Six-year old Tottie just stood by and watched while all the boys picked fruits in silence, rapidly filling their mouths, pockets and wherever they had room for them in their clothes. Anda crept noiselessly from branch to branch and the wiry Dexter swung up in the fork of the tree where the biggest and pinkest *tambis* grew. Japheth and Guiller scooped up the fruits that had fallen on the ground. Dark-skinned and white-toothed Mawie munched on the sweet, juicy *tambis* as he scrambled up the tree like a black monkey or *aliwas* in the forest of Claver, Surigao del Norte. Everyone was quick on his feet as there was no minute to lose. The excitement was tremendous.

Grandmother's Tambis Tree, Christina Buo, 2015.

The tambis tree in my grandparents' garden bears shiny pink fruits in the summer month of May.

Andy peered fearfully through the dark and quiet street. He continued to look straight ahead until he saw something white moving slowly out of the shadows. He saw someone approaching. He called out in a voice loud enough for the boys to hear, *"Pssst!* Hurry! Somebody's coming!"

He flashed his light towards it and gasped in horror at what he saw. Andy's face turned white and his blood froze at that moment. Never in his life had he seen anything like it. Visible in the moonlight, perhaps ten feet away, a woman in white with long black hair, floated towards him.

"Nag-uno man kamo did-on?" (What are you doing there?) asked the woman from nobody knows where.

Andy sprang to his feet and fled. The rest of the boys peered through the green leaves of the *tambis* to see whose voice it was that spoke to them. They were struck dumb when they saw a faceless, ghostly figure of a woman dressed in white, standing in the corner of the street. All at once there was panic and in a minute, they jumped down from the tree, scrambled up onto the wall and bolted down the street. Wax apples inside their shirts and pockets tumbled down around them.

The boys came running at full speed; there were no voices, no shouting. They passed by us, and instinctively we followed them, a real horror of fear running over us like a rippling wave.

Finally, we stopped and stood against the wooden post or *haligi* of the *nipa* hut[19] of our neighbors, *Tia* Bunding and her husband, *Tio* Benjamin and family. We were as badly scared as the boys.

"What made you run off like that? It looks as if you had just seen a monster," we asked our cousins.

In the 1980s, the Petromax lamp was one of the
sources of light in rural Philippines.

It must have been a real shock for when Roy tried to say something, nothing came out. He and his brothers were too frightened and distracted to speak. It was already midnight when we reached home and hurried anxiously upstairs.

Our grandmother came out of her room, obviously disturbed by the commotion we made.

"What has happened? What is all this about? What are you children doing up at this hour of the night?" *Lola* Deding inquired.

So there we were, by the lamplight, in the lonely dead of midnight, sitting around the dining table with *Lola*, listening to the brothers, Roy, Ronald and Randy tell us about the tale of the White Lady. As they recounted the incident, we felt the same sick horrible feeling of fear that they had experienced. We were not only frightened but also thrilled at the same time, by the mystery and horror of the White Lady.

"Who was this woman?" we asked *Lola*.

Who was she? What is she? Had this woman come back from the other realm in search of something or someone? Could she be a lost, tormented soul wandering the four corners of the world, pining for the love she left behind or perhaps weeping for a love lost? Had she had come back to claim a promise or make atonement? What is the mystery of this woman in white who haunts the dark streets on a bewitching moonlight night?

"Nobody really knows. Maybe it's the spirit who watches over the *tambis* tree in your *Lolo* Ores' garden. Now children, you better wash now. It's time to go to bed," *Lola* said, shooing us off the table, "Remember always that you must never sneak around your neighbor's garden at midnight."

Silence is as sweet as a tide's kiss on the shore,
it helps me hear God's whisper
in my bewilderment,
comforts me in my pain,
extols me in my feat
and keeps me company
in solitude.

* Maria Sherrylyn Buo -Sigman

Sunrise in Dapa, Siargao Island.

Photo: Christina Buo

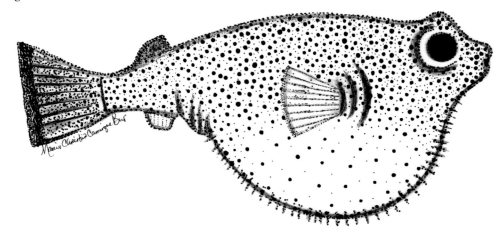

My First Pufferfish

One of the things we liked doing most during the summer was going on an excursion to our grandparents' beach house in Camangahit in Malinao, just one kilometer southwest of the *poblacion* or town center. Summer was one endless adventure after another and the lagoon, glittering with all the blue of sapphire and all the sparkle of the sun, caressed by all the fragrance of the fresh summer breeze, was our paradise.

We lived in *Purok* 2 (*Dos*)[1] in General Luna, with our grandparents, parents, aunts, uncles and cousins for all the childhood summers we spent in Siargao Island. And it was summer that usually drove the whole family down to the Camangahit Beach for a picnic. Under the cool shade of the swaying coconut palms, the solitary house by the beach would come alive once again, in the summer.

It was a small paradise unto itself, the Camangahit beach house,
very secluded, open to the winds and fronting the bluest blue lagoon.

My five siblings, Maie, Marjo, Elaine, Josephus, Mashelle and several cousins and I woke up from our daily, obligatory *siesta*[2] and rushed out of the house, whooping and sliding down the stair-rail and out the door, letting out gleeful shouts into the street, where all our friends and relatives were eagerly waiting for us.

The quickest way to Camangahit is down a sand road that leads southwest of *Purok Uno* (1) in the town proper, towards the neighboring village of Malinao, one of 19 *barangays*[3] of General Luna, on the eastern coast of Siargao Island. It was exciting hiking through the town and into the woods with our lively troop. There were more than a dozen of us, nimble and tireless boys and girls, from 5 years to 15 years of age, walking jauntily along that sandy road one hot summer afternoon.

Pied fantails twittered and darted among trees. Gauzy-winged butterflies and humming, metallic dragonflies hovered over wildflowers and green ferns, sometimes alighting on the grass that grows by the wayside. Grasshoppers jump away whenever we try to catch them. We continued along the path, bordered by *papaya, atis*[4] *caimito*[5], *mayambago* and coconut palms. Now and then we meet a farmer riding on a cart drawn by a *carabao*[6]. Some others walk barefoot, wearing a *sarok*[7] with a *buyo* or a *sundang*[8] hanging on the waistband. We passed by two small, swarthy boys, in tattered clothes, their shoulders bent as they lugged home dry twigs, fallen branches, driftwood from the beach, for kindling fires or *pang-sugnod*.

Through the window of a little *nipa*[9] hut, we could see a mother gently rocking her baby to sleep, in a *buwa*[10].

As we strode along Bongayon, Jose Roy turned to his cousin, Maie. "Don't you know? His eyes widened in wonder. "That's the haunted hill of Daruhan, which belongs to your daddy!"

Maie shuddered at the thought. Jose Roy pointed to a small round hill on the right, so densely covered in wild vegetation scrambling among rocks and misshapen trees. Folks living at the foot of the hill could hear strange voices and the laughter of invisible little children playing in the backyard around midnight. Once, a mother and her children were wakened in the wee hours by the sound of a dreadful thud on the *bubong* or roof and the flapping of great wings directly over their heads which so frightened them that they huddled together on the *baliu*[11] *banig* or sleeping-mat and prayed.

Maie plays with a blue butterfly in Camangahit.

23

A feeling of horror came upon us as we looked at the haunted-looking hill. Our friend, Leonila, and her several brothers and sisters often went up the hill to pick the beans of the cacao trees. Her grandmother would then roast and grind the cacao beans to make aromatic and natural coffee or *kape*.

"Somebody told me we're entering the domain of a witch who can turn herself into a strange pig or dog, or whatever form she likes, and suddenly appears inside other people's homes after midnight -"

Jose Roy never finished all that he wanted to say. We were all frightened now and our hearts were beating loudly. Instinctively we ran as fast and as hard as we could, down the road, jumping over rocks and stray logs, far, far away from that wretched witch's enclave until we found ourselves approaching near the Camangahit beach house, breathless tired and thirsty.

"*Tia* Tura! *Tia* Tura! *Tia* Tura!"

We called to our smiling and friendly caretaker, Artura, whom we found by the *atabay*[12] pulling up a dripping bucket of water. She looked up and smiled at us.

"Would you like something to drink?" she asked us.

"It's a long walk from the town," she said as she led all of us into the kitchen and scooped up pure, cold water out of the *banga* or earthen jar and poured it in tin cups for us to drink. The water never tasted better!

The place was a small paradise unto itself, open to the winds, and very secluded. The nearest neighbor was two kilometers away. It was an idyllic spot, the Camangahit beach house, nestling under a coconut grove and fronting a white beach lapping the blue lagoon. A Bermuda grass garden, with

COCONUT
Cocos nucifera
Niyug or lubi

marigold blossoms and fragrant *kalachuchi*[13] was a labor of love from my hard-working, green-thumbed grandmother, Josefina, or *Lola* Deding.

There was a spare kitchen and an airy *sala*[14] in the ground floor. Upstairs there were two fairly-sized rooms, looking out into tall and full-grown coconut palm trees. One of my favorite things to do here is swinging in the *abaca*[15] hammock hanging between two big *molave* posts.

25

On the ground level, there were conspicuous letters, I and D, hand-painted on opposite walls facing the beach. Letter I stood for Indong, my maternal grandfather, and the letter D, for my grandmother, Deding. They had it built in 1955, and this gracious summer house had known good days and bad. It gradually fell into disrepair and ruinous decay. The house no longer exists but it is woven inextricably in the vivid memories of our carefree and happy childhood summers.

Summers in Camangahit, oil by Christina Buo.

Jose Roy

Ann-ann

Ryan

Jun-jun   Christina

Elaine   Mashelle   Maie   26

here stretching before us is the broad expanse of the lagoon, sparkling like gold and blue silk in the bright sunlight. There is the secluded Janoyoy Island with haunted caves and populated with wild birds. The tide was ebbing and shell-catchers were foraging the shallows for edible *tagitis*, *kinhason*[16] and *tajum* or sea urchin.

Jopee   Marjo   Ivy   Doris

christina Buc

The boys ran down to the shallow water, carrying their empty cans and bottles to stock the fishes and baby shrimp. They were going fishing, using their shirts as nets. I watched them roll up their trousers and take off their shirts as they wade in the low water, skimming for *ibis, dumod-ot, ito* and *agak*[17].

The outgoing tide had exposed the *lusay*[18] or seagrass and rock pools teeming with small fishes and baby shrimp. The boys hunted among the rocks crusted with *lumot* and groped about for fishes proliferating on the green filamentous algae.

Summer in the island gathered to a scorching tropical heat. Some girls stayed in the shade, especially those who were afraid of the sun. My elder sister, Marjo, had become wary of the sun for fear it will darken her already dusky complexion. Despite the breathless and burning heat of May, I combed the beach and poked among sea shells and

We ran about the beach and frolicked under the May sunshine until our skin burned and we went home darker but healthier and happier than ever.

pebbles in the sand. As it often happens after spending the summer in the great outdoors on the island, we return to Cebu City with fresh vigor and sunburned skin. On the first day of school, our classmates could hardly recognize us for we looked so dark only our teeth and uniform were visible to the human eye.

I looked around and saw the boys - my brother, Tottie, cousins Ryan, Roy, Randy, Ronald, Ken, Ian-*maro*, Lalo-ay, Pierre Lou, Lloyd, Jun-jun, and our friends, the twins Jodel and Rodel, Mawie, Anda, Punat, Dexter, Bulutong and Eric, far away in the tide. I began to wade carefully along the edge of the lagoon, lifting my skirt. The water was warm and shallow and reached below my knees. Then I came to a pool swarming with tiny silvery fishes, shining like mirror in the sunlight. I tried to scoop them out, but they slipped through my fingers. I peered through the clear water and found starfish and brittle stars in the waving grass.

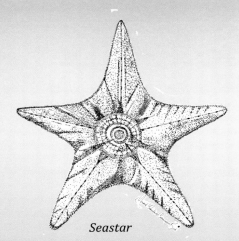

Seastar

Then, out of the blue, a dark, mischievous girl named Langga came up behind me and planted a squirming brittle star on my head! *Arrgh!* I was so enraged but she fled before I could get my hands on her!

After a while I saw something swimming slowly nearby. My heart pounding, I eagerly watched and stalked a medium-sized, box-like fish meandering slowly in the shallows, its short, thick, beautifully-marked body, swelling and puffing itself into a prickly ball. Such a fish! It was so much bigger than the tiny *dumod-ot* or *agak*, the usual catch of the boys which are very common in these parts.

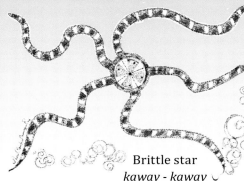

Brittle star
kaway - kaway

It looked docile and moved in a sluggish manner; its spotted body stood out against the white sand, with black, brown and white patterns and bulging eyes; out of its sides grew pectoral fins and its white stomach stretched out stiff, with hair-like spines. I thought it was the finest, however strange and unique-looking, fish I ever saw in my life! I drew near it, carefully and nervously. A slow-swimming fish was an easy target. I have never caught fish before but I'll give it a fair shot!

Imitating the boys, I removed my blouse and held it as a throwing net. I was nine years old and didn't care if the sun burned my arms or my back. I waded stealthily, in crouching position, then dipped my blouse into the water and spread it beneath the ballooning fish. I waited for a few seconds then I gathered it carefully at the edges, scooping the fish from the water.

"I caught something! I caught a fish!" I shouted excitedly.

My eight-year-old cousin, Ryan, came running down the shore towards me.

"What did you find?"

I proudly showed it to him and he said, laughing, "It's a *butete!*"

It was a pufferfish[19], also called bubblefish, globefish, balloonfish or toadfish. It is locally known as *butete* in Siargao Island. It was bigger than the size of the palm of one's hand.

Ryan took the pufferfish that I had caught and thrust into my hand his Coke bottle filled with hundreds of tiny fishes!

"It's poisonous. You can't eat it. You're going to die if you do. Here, you can have mine if you let me take that," Ryan suggested, obviously jealous.

Before I could even say anything, he took the pufferfish that I had caught and thrust into my hand his 1 liter glass Coke bottle filled with hundreds of tiny *dumod-ot!*

I do not know whether it was a fair deal or not, but it did not really matter. I was overjoyed to find an exotic creature and to catch it all by myself! I went home feeling proud and exultant as an explorer, floating on air, that day I caught a fish for the very first time.

The sea beckons me,
dispels depression
forgets furies,
dampens worries
and keeps me afloat
in the welter of hope.

* Maria Sherrylyn Buo -Sigman

Baybay, Burgos,
Siargao Island.

Photo: Melvin Tiu Comahig

Seraphim, the Turtle-Dove

When I was 17, a friend of my brother, Josephus, gave me a tiny *tukmo*[1]. I took him with me everywhere I went in my parents' hometown in General Luna, Siargao Island, where I had spent most of my carefree childhood summers. When it was time to leave and go back to school in Cebu City, I kissed my bird goodbye. As I gently patted his wings, a single feather dropped into my hand and I have kept it to this day, between the covers of a red notebook.

Seraphim, as I named the juvenile turtle-dove, was so tiny and tame, he snuggled up easily in my cupped hand. He did not chirp. He had not found his voice yet. His feathers are brown and gray color; his glance soft and curious as he tilts his head and looks up at me with those trustful, little jet-black eyes, twinkling like stars. How could I not fall under the spell of this fragile and fascinating creature that nestled quietly in the palm of my hand?

I cuddled him against my chest as I carried him to the room or *kuarto* vacated by my Uncle Franklin in our ancestral home. I set a place for him on the bedside table and everyday he has corn and grains of rice. At first, he would not eat. So I tied a string around his leg and wrapped the loose end around my index finger so I could be at his side until at last he ate grain seeds from my hand.

Seraphim soon became my best bird friend that summer. I would wake up at dawn, scoop him into my hand, dash out the door, skip up and down the *plaza,*[2] pass through the garden of *Gmelina* trees, in the Central Elementary school grounds and run gaily towards the beautiful beach.

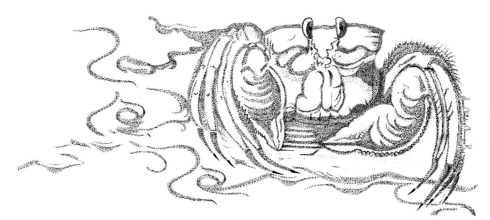

GHOST CRAB
Karaykay

It only takes less than five minutes to get to the beach from our house in the *poblacion*[3]. Here, I spend the summer mornings watching the spectacular sunrise, feeling the gentle sea breeze caress my face, walking barefoot on the sand and finding *karaykay* or ghost crabs, Moon shell scallops, common Indo-Pacific cowries, shining brown seaweeds, fossils of sea urchins and occasionally, tiny blue bubbles of the dangerous Portuguese man-of-war washed ashore.

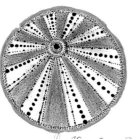

Shells of the burrowing sea urchin, locally called saluaki.

34

The white beach of General Luna faces the east, overlooking a white-sand lagoon laid out like a shining mirror of sapphire, emerald and silver. The white-sand coastline stretches from Malinao in the south all the way to Santa Fe and Santa Cruz in the north. Sitting here beneath the shade of a *talisay* or Indian almond tree, I love to contemplate the islands of Guyam, Daku and Janoyoy, and the breakers plunging merrily and perpetually upon the *Pisangan* barrier reef. Native sailboats or *lajag* drift across the horizon. Boys race across the beach tossing their *tabanog*[4] in the wind. Brahminy kites, locally called *banog*, winged their way into the air.

On the horizon, the frothing white breakers from the Pacific plunge unceasingly upon the Pisangan Barrier Reef in the town of General Luna.

All through the sunny month of May, we did everything in twos. I would ride my bike along the white-sand streets with Seraphim perched on my shoulder. Sometimes I take him along as I pick flowers for the altars at home – bright red Prince Charming blossoms, sunny cosmos, bitter-smelling marigolds, pink *gumamela*[5] and magenta blooms of bougainvillea.

I was always thrilled to spend more time with Seraphim, petting him, talking and singing to him, hand-feeding him. He had, as weeks went by, charmed his way into our hearts. Some afternoons I would find my youngest sister, Mashelle, who shares the same interest in birds, napping in my bed, her finger tied to the leg of Seraphim, lying still beside her. He lit up the whole household and amused my uncle who kept domestic pigeons in a cote built high up on a post across the street.

I dreaded only one thing. I did not want to take Seraphim anywhere near my cousin, Peter Ryan, or his fierce-looking pet iguana for fear it might gobble him up. He lived next door and was very fond of hunting creatures for mere sport and did not share my romantic view of birds at all.

I insisted Seraphim stay close to me. But trouble began one day when my little bird finally fluttered his wings and flew from my hand high up towards the uppermost branches of the grotesque *Dap-dap*[6] tree, while we were strolling on the beachside school grounds. It caught me completely off guard!

All at once - my younger cousin, Fabian Carlo, whom we called Chuck-chuck, climbed up the *Dap-dap* and in quick leaps, stood on the trunk of the tree, staring into the knotted branches, hoping to catch Seraphim for me.

"Chuuuuck, come down! You might fall off the tree!" Chuck's older sister, Den-den, cried out.

She yelled at him again and looked appealingly at her brother who said nothing but leapt to the ground and alighted before us. I sighed, and wondered if I would ever see my bird again. I know I should let Seraphim fly free. After all, birds belong to the open skies and sunshine.

But I wasn't ready to let him go just yet. My heart was bound to him. I knew it would be almost impossible to find Seraphim. There were so many places he could be. He could be flying across the water or gone back to the forest. How could I persuade him to come to me?

I enlisted the help of my younger siblings, Elaine, Tottie, Mashelle, our cousins and friends and we fanned out like a search party in the school grounds, calling out Seraphim's name into every bush and tree, our voices echoing through the air.

S e r a p h i m!   *S e r a p h i m!*   *S e r a p h i m!*

"Phim, Phim," answered the echo.

Without realizing it, our search had taken us towards the shoreline of *Purok 3*, just across the General Luna National High School. We redoubled our efforts, calling out his name a hundred times, peering up into coconut trees, asking the birds and even the air around us. I was praying and hoping Seraphim would come home on my voice.

Seraphim!   *Seraphim!*   *Seraphim!*

"Phim, Phim," replied the echo.

Suddenly, I seemed to hear or feel something rustle at my feet, among the leaves of the thick underbrush. I looked down, and there, partially hidden among the bright-green patches of the sprawling beach *lambajong* shrub and its tangled mass of vine stems, was my bird, Seraphim!

"You came back," I whispered softly to him as I knelt down beside him and stroked his side. I knew him by the string that I wrapped around his spindly leg which was still hanging there. Then I lifted him up and gave him a kiss. It was a miracle. Seraphim returned.

"I found him! I found him! I found Seraphim!" I shouted to everybody and they all came running eagerly to me from all directions, jumping for joy over the little bird that was lost and found.

Christina Camingue Buo

LIFE
Divine gift
Fraught with prodigious love
Amazing breath
Forthwith it gushes.

Behold earth
Creature blest
Thou hast been drawn
From God's bosom.

But fie! A world
of halo and horn
of scowl and smile
Unveils unto thine.

Rapt in beauty
Thy soul dances
Joy of beyond
Thou fly aloft.

A ruthless contradiction
chary of justice
As the poor trudges
While the rich rides.

It does prick hard
with every banished dream
every stolen hope
encompassed in thy heart.

Oh life! So perplexing.
Thy mind pines away
so precarious
Thou art petrified.

Hail God
with thy sweet entreatment
That thou be clad
in His gentlest embrace.

A heavenly serenade
lulls spirit thine
And suddenly
comes life sublime.

Silhouette of a large-billed black crow or *uwak*.
Tawin-Tawin, General Luna.
Photo: Christina Buo

* Maria Sherrylyn Buo-Sigman

The Portuguese Man-of-War

Elaine remembers that morning very well. She could see the beautiful blue sky, studded with wispy, cotton clouds and the white tossing rim of the waves from the Pacific breaking in over the *Pisangan Reef* [1]. She could feel the cool wind on her face, fingering through her short brown hair and caressing with the gentle breath of summer. She could smell the damp sand, the seaweeds, the salty breeze and the leaves of the green, growing trees. She could hear the voices and laughter of her cousins, Maryrose and Phoebelyn, as they walk excitedly down the beach on this windy May morning in General Luna, Siargao Island.

Summer is the best season in Siargao; it is family picnics under the trees during a *copra* [2] harvest; rambles along rough roads dusty in the sun and through the woods; running barefoot in the summer rain; pulling paper boats along the water in the puddle; hunting for bird's nests and drifting on a *lajag* [3] at sunset; singing and dancing on the beach to The Culture Club's Karma Chameleon and the music of the 1980s on the portable radio; it is diving off the wooden jetty and skinny-dipping by the light of the moon and the stars.

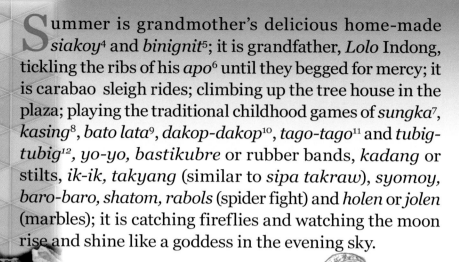

Summer is grandmother's delicious home-made *siakoy*[4] and *binignit*[5]; it is grandfather, *Lolo* Indong, tickling the ribs of his *apo*[6] until they begged for mercy; it is carabao sleigh rides; climbing up the tree house in the plaza; playing the traditional childhood games of *sungka*[7], *kasing*[8], *bato lata*[9], *dakop-dakop*[10], *tago-tago*[11] and *tubig-tubig*[12], *yo-yo, bastikubre* or rubber bands, *kadang* or stilts, *ik-ik, takyang* (similar to *sipa takraw*), *syomoy, baro-baro, shatom, rabols* (spider fight) and *holen* or *jolen* (marbles); it is catching fireflies and watching the moon rise and shine like a goddess in the evening sky.

Summer is picking fresh flowers and offering them with prayers and songs to the Blessed Virgin Mary during *Flores de Mayo*[13]. Every afternoon in the month of May, young boys and girls in the town would go off for long walks and gather flowers of all kinds - *kampanilya* (yellow bell), *kalachuchi*, yellow cosmos, perfumed *ylang-ylang, dama de noche*, fleur-de-lis, *adgao* and *mayambago* blossoms, wild santan, violet, pink and white *bukingan*, the edible blossoms of the flaming fire tree or *arbol de fuego*, red *tapulanga, gumamela*, bougainvillea and sunflower in the neighboring gardens, along the creek or *sapa-sapa* in Mabua, Bongbong, Malinao and over the hills of Tawin-tawin.

The church bells ring at 3 o'clock for the *Flores de Mayo*, ting tong, ting tong, resounding over the small, parochial town, and every boy and girl, dressed in white or clad in their best clothes, carry colorful bouquets, wreaths and baskets of flowers and walk by twos in one long line from the entrance down to the central aisle towards the front pews of the *simbahan* or church.

Inside, the youth and the *cantora*[14] raise their eager voices together in singing traditional Marian hymns, chants and religious songs without instrumental accompaniment. When the devotion is almost over, the children sprinkle colorful petals on the statue of the Blessed Virgin Mary, singing *Flores a Maria*:

> *Venid y vamos todos con flores a porfia*
> *con flores a Maria que Madre nuestra es*
> *con flores a Maria que Madre nuestra es*

Slowly, streams of children filed out of the church, singing with all of their heart and soul.

> *Adto na kami Maria*
> *Adios kanimo, Señora*
> *Ug ayaw kami hikalimti, sa kadautan panlabani*
> *Adto Na kami, Adios, Maria, Adios, Adios, kanimo, Señora*[15]

The Maytime heritage devotion culminates in the *Santacruzan*, where townfolks join a traditional, religious procession, commemorating the finding of the Holy Cross of Christ in Calvary by *Reyna Elena* or Empress St. Helena, mother of the Roman Emperor Constantine, with a parade of *zagalas* or young ladies representing biblical and historical characters.

Christina Camingue Buo

Island-hopping to Guyam Island by
Christina Buo

44

Summer is also for swimming. It is the season of the year when the lagoon in General Luna is a gorgeous mantle of rippling blue-green, stretching far away in the horizon. One could spend time from dawn to dusk, getting around in the water, beneath or by the edge of the water, and have a simply perfect day.

The three cousins, Elaine, Maryrose and Phoebelyn, ran down to the lagoon, the tide was high so they jumped at once in the water, white-whipped by a summer wind. Oh, what pure joy and enchantment! The beauty of the islands, the open skies, the pearly morning light, the tangy breeze, the tweeting birds and the swaying trees all exploded around them!

The beach was empty and it seemed to belong to them. It was as if no other world existed and they were bathing in the waters of their own Lagoon of Eden, a flowing, floating fairyland far away from the ordinary world. No swim was ever better than when there were no crowds. It was like a fresh, new awakening, nature's benediction. New life rushes back into the veins and one feels refreshed, renewed and reborn.

Then suddenly, out of nowhere, there came dozens and dozens of oddly fascinating, iridescent, purple-blue balloon-like creatures, about as big as the palm of the hand, sailing before the wind and drifting along with the current, and the girls found themselves amidst a whole fleet of beautiful but dangerous Portuguese men- of- war.

Floating on the water's surface, they look like tiny fishing boats with smooth and shiny azure, pink or purple sails, the crested diagonal floats of the man-of-war. But underneath the water, the Portuguese man–of-war's long, dangling tentacles can deliver a sting and paralyze fish and other small organisms, for food.

Maryrose was so astonished by these jellyfish-like creatures that she tried to pick them, but Elaine and Phoebelyn turned away from the venomous invertebrates and swam back to the shore.

"Look at these cute things, floating like blue bubbles!" said Maryrose and she put out her hand to touch them.

When they headed back home, only a short walk from the beach, Maryrose suddenly felt a painful, burning sensation passing through her body. She was feeling dizzy and began gasping for breath. Everything started to grow dark and blank.

"I feel like being electrocuted," she complained.

At the ancestral home, the girls rushed upstairs to the *pantaw* or open back porch, where they wash after swimming, each taking turns pumping water from their favorite, old-fashioned hand pump. As soon as they laid Maryrose down in a wooden chair, she rolled back her eyes and collapsed.

"What happened?" Uncle Ben pushed the kitchen door open and burst into the *pantaw* suddenly.

"She got stung by the *tayuha*," replied Elaine, looking pale and restrained, scared at what was happening to her cousin. She began to pray, "Lord, please don't let her die."

Phoebelyn, Uncle Ben's daughter, was fanning Maryrose vigorously, in an effort to revive her.

They called on Rochelle, the teen-age house help, who came quickly, bringing a bowl of freshly-squeezed coconut milk or *gata*, the local folks' potent remedy for hydroid stings. Others also use vinegar or *suka*, *calamansi*[16], *sabila* or aloe vera, and rub or apply it in the affected area. In about fifteen minutes, Maryrose regained consciousness and found Rochelle bending over her, rubbing her fingers and nullifying the poisonous sting in her hands with warm coconut milk. All of them breathed a sigh of relief. She was very fortunate to survive.

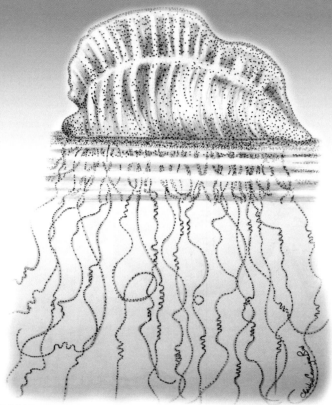

PORTUGUESE MAN-OF-WAR
Physalia species
Tayuha

In all their growing years spent together summering in the island, the girls have never encountered such a dazzlingly beautiful but notorious creature of the sea. Fisherfolks say these creatures appear in numbers on a windy day, coming into shallow water or stranding on beaches. Adverse winds and peculiar current patterns bring together a number of these strange coelenterates close to the shore. The man-of-war's poisonous tentacles dangle in the water like long strings waiting to sting the hapless human bathers or capture the creatures that cross its path.

Bathers must be forewarned, Elaine thought, pausing at the edge of the sun-swept lagoon. After the incident, the cousins gained a new-found respect for the Portuguese man-of-war, which should be carefully avoided, just like the deadly box jelly or *sayabay* (sea wasp).

"We must always be wary at sea. We can never be too sure of our own safety," Elaine murmured, striding across the sand toward the clear green water where her cousins were waiting for her.

I was hollow as naught,
but Your Love
gave me substance
enough to mold
my priceless worth.

* Maria Sherrylyn Buo- Sigman

Jesus' Face in Calvary (Black & White Ink, Pencil) by Josephus C. Buo

Firefly Dances

Iwould never forget that evening of fireflies, February 13. It was one of those perfect tropical nights, cool, crisp and clear. There was a blackout in the town as my mother, Evelyn, and I set out together on the pitch-dark street to visit our relatives and farm workers in the *poblacion*[1]. Overhead, a million stars smiled down on us and we enjoyed the feel of the fresh salty breeze, rustling the *kalachuchi*[2] trees near the Mother Mary grotto at the Santo Tomas De Villanueva Parish Church[3]. Several minutes later, we came to the *bahay kubo*[4] of *Tio* Macario and his wife, *Tia* Doring in *Purok* 5.

The *bahay kubo* was illuminated by the faint glow of a *lamparilla*[5] and they spoke in hushed voices so as not to disturb the neighbors as well as the hens, which were fast asleep in the coop underneath the hut. I waited for my mother outside where I could only hear, but not see, the frogs croaking and the crickets chirping in the backyard. As my eyes adapted to the dark, I was astonished to see a synchronous flashing of what looked like living stars lighting up a huge tree. Off to the left, among other plants and trees, stood a *kolo*, from which presently tiny pinpoints of white-yellow light blinked in and out. The breadfruit tree bedecked itself with hundreds and hundreds of *kipat-kipat* glowing like jewels in the dark. I was stunned. I stood there motionless and speechless. It was as if a fairy wand was waved before my eyes and I was caught in a starry spell.

Under the Full Moon, Manuel Pañares, 2015.

"What are you peering out for? It's getting late and it's time we started for home," mother looked puzzled as she called out for me at the *hagdan* or stairs of the *bahay kubo*.

I did not appear to notice or hear her until after she called my name for the third time. I stood there transfixed by the spectacular nocturnal display of fireflies, blinking by the hundreds, or thousands, in the huge *kolo*. All the mystery and magic of that February night seemed to have gathered there amid the outlines of the spreading breadfruit tree.

We turned in at half past nine - my mom, my eldest sister and I, lying in bed, cuddled in between grandmother's soft, blankets, feeling the comfort of her crisp, clean, white cotton sheets and pillows that smelled of fresh soap. *Lola* Deding's room is elegantly furnished with a solid wood, vintage boudoir dresser or *tokador,* with a large mirror, dark wooden cabinet or *aparador* and an elaborate altar, with a white crucifix sculpture, images of the Sacred Heart of Jesus, The Holy Child Jesus or *Santo Niño,* The Blessed Virgin Mary, Saint Joseph, pictures of the Holy Family, fresh flowers in a vase, vials of holy oil, votive candles and an oil lamp that burned day and night.

The room looks west into our neighbor's backyard and overlooks a full-grown breadfruit tree. Some of the curtained, glazed sliding windows were still open and I heard the chorus of crickets and notes of the frogs outside. Inside the ancestral house, there was scarcely a sound to be heard except the relentless tick, tock, tick, tock of the Grandfather clock.

Shortly after we had gone to bed, I noticed a tiny yellow light pulsating from one firefly that appeared in the ceiling directly above me. Slowly at first, it went round and round, then began spinning faster and faster like a wheel, forming luminous circles of light. Then it stops and the glow becomes faint, before finally disappearing in the dark. Suddenly, it switches its light again. Then it goes off and on again, not so very bright now. Sometimes, it would light up for just a moment and then fade away.

Night of Fireflies and Falling Stars, pen and ink stippling by Christina Buo, 2015.

I gasped in astonishment as I watched the exquisite dance of the firefly. From night until dawn, I would open my eyes half-consciously to find the firefly still winking at me on the same spot in the ceiling. I never felt quite the same since then. This was the beginning of my extraordinary encounters with a friendly firefly I call *Fira*.

When I returned four months later, she showed up again. It was the eve of my departure to the city. I was lying in bed with my grandmother, *Lola* Deding, now fast asleep, when I saw a flickering firefly suspended in the ceiling, directly above my head. Sometimes *Fira* would show up the night of my arrival or the last night before my departure.

Once, I thought she followed me straight into the house that day I came to town. A firefly floated past me as my friends and neighbors, Melanie, Marifi, Madel and I went for a sunset stroll down the wooden jetty. When I reached the house and went up to my dusky room, I saw a tiny spot of light blinking from one firefly who clung like a shadow to the window glass pane, creating a mysteriously beautiful effect in the dark.

I have thrilled to moments like seeing a *talisay* tree on the beach lit up by a glittering multitude of fireflies as I go biking on the shore at dusk. When the moon is out of sight,fireflies make hauntingly beautiful shows, winking by the dozens or hundreds, on the *mayambago* and *talisay* trees in Daku and Anajawan Islands, encircling the white flowering *panumboyon* and *adgao* trees on the beach in the island village of La Januza, creeping along the damp rice paddies and flying over the mangrove swamp in Tawin - Tawin.

Dancing Fireflies, Christina Buo, 2015.

Thousands of "kipat-kipat" or fireflies light up the talisay tree as I bike along the quiet beach at dusk.

In the starlight, they gather, in glittering profusion, around the leaves and branches of the white flowering *adgao,* in the *katunggan*[6], lighting it up like a fairy Christmas tree. No sound is heard but the ethereal beauty of fireflies casts a spell and weaves shimmering white magic around us.

Christina Camingue Buo

Fireflies rival the beauty of stars, and on one such evening in October, lent a sense of magic in the air.

We were enjoying a despedida party at a beachside bar for my cousin, Ivy Floryvic, and her friends, Joyleen and Catherine, from Surigao City when I stepped outside for a breath of sea air.

"Catch them if you can."

The voice came out of nowhere. I turned around and saw a tall, lean yet muscular, rugged-looking Australian, with a shaven head and large, piercing blue eyes, standing next to me on the beach.

"They're very elusive, " I replied.

We stood talking to each other in the shadow of the *talisay* tree where fireflies flitted about and basked in the cool night air. There was a balmy onshore breeze and the lagoon was the color of silver-indigo by moonlight. Here and there, fireflies gleamed like joyous little sprites, a shower of sparks and light upon us, weaving their magic, melting the ice of cold reserve and breaking down walls of formality between two strangers.

Twilight over the Lagoon, Christina Buo, 2013.
Collection of Jieve Gantuangco.

There was also one special evening I could not forget. My friends from Cebu, Fe Emlyn and Sybil and I were going to spend the night at my Aunt Ada's cottage on the edge of a cliff in Catangnan, about two kilometers from the town proper. Her son, Pierre Lou, invited us to stay overnight in their cliff-top rest house in what was then called Tuazon Fairview Point. He joined us earlier in the day as we went exploring the secluded beaches and huge rocks at the bottom of the cliff. In the distance, three wave-washed rock islands, "The Rocks", stand like sentinels of the sea and Cloud Nine surfing rollers pour in straight from the Pacific. Here in this enchanting spot, we could fall asleep to the rhythm of the waves and wake up to the cheery chirping of birds, the sea wind blowing in our faces and a great, flaming sunrise to start our day!

At present, this is the site of the miraculous shrine of The Glorious Cross of Love - *Ang Mahimayaong Krus sa Gugma*. This sacred sanctuary was a dream realized in 2005 by my Aunt Doris, who blazed trails as the first lady lawyer of Siargao (1965) as well as its first lady mayor when President Cory Aquino appointed her OIC Mayor of General Luna in 1986. She had the shrine built with the help and support of her equally devout and generous sisters, Lina, a histotechnologist, who had been in practice in Oakpark, Illinois, USA, and Bernarda (Ada), who worked as a stenographer at the Court of the First Instance in Dapa. It has been said that since the Glorious Cross was built on top of the cliff, the town has been saved from severe typhoons and calamities.

Fifteen minutes later, we ascended the dim path to my aunts' property. It was a long wooded land, surrounded by tall coconut palms, the house at the end of it. It was very difficult to locate the house because of the dark shade of trees.

Everything seemed to be drowned in total darkness. All of the people had gone indoors, and they probably turned in early for the night for I couldn't see any light. But it was only eight o' clock in the evening!

I led my friends, Fe Emlyn and Sybil into a thick grove of coconut trees, their palm fronds arched gracefully still and silent into the air, casting a mantle of shadow and mystery all around us. It was a dark, moonless night. We walked very close together and hurried along the path. We had no weapon except our faith and courage against the powers and principalities of darkness.

"Are there snakes around here?" Fe Emlyn asked.

"I hope not. I never heard of it."

I tried to assuage her fears because she was terrified at the thought of snakes lurking in the grass or rocks and traps hidden underground. Shortly afterward, we found ourselves walking blindly into a low wall, overlooking a glass house on a cliff.

"Is that it?" Sybil pointed to the dream house.

"No. I think that one belongs to an Australian," I said to them as we gazed admiringly at the dream house on a cliff-top.

We were lost in the middle of the dark woods and it was difficult to decide exactly where to go next but we turned back and went on together a little farther until presently we perceived a light flickering from a distance. Then I heard my aunt, *Mama Ada*, calling out to me from the dark silhouette of the house at the edge of the trees.

"Is that you, Christina? Mind your step. It's very dark."

As we walked towards the house, one flickering firefly floated in our midst. I paused, reached out for her with my left hand and whispered, *Fira*.

To my surprise and amazement, she alighted on my finger! For a moment, I felt its cold light on my hand. I felt a strong affection and an extraordinary connection with that one glimmering firefly.

What's more magical than a night sky full of falling stars and fireflies dancing in the summer breeze?

"It's like a scene out of a Disney movie," exclaimed my friend, Fe Emlyn, who saw what happened.

The rest of the evening was idyllic; shooting stars, like divine blessings, fell from the sky; Fe Emlyn, Sybil and I nestled snug in our *abaca*[7] hammocks, hung beneath the shade of the trees, where fireflies frolicked in the breeze.

Fireflies have shown me something that was real and not make-believe. It is an extraordinary friendship. I love fireflies and the feeling, I might say, is mutual. In the witching hour of a tropical summer night, the enchantment of one and a thousand fireflies fell over me.

Christina Camingue Buo

Ensconced in my reveries
And bewinged over the moon

At the sound of YOUR whisper.

* Maria Sherrylyn Buo - Sigman

Flaming sunset in Sta. Monica, Siargao Island.

Photo: Sol Antoinette Tiu Andanar

Once upon a time, there was a little girl quite unlike any other. Folks in the farming village of Consuelo called her *kabog* for she strangely resembled the nocturnal mammal – the bat.

Lucita and her family lived in a *bahay kubo*[1] near the school in Consuelo, a farming village west of the General Luna town proper. Most families here eke out a living from the land. The forests that cover the village's mountainous, gently rolling terrain are habitats for the *kayaw* or Rufous hornbill, *banog* or Brahminy kite, *amag* or Philippine tarsier[2] and *kabog* or the giant flying fox[3]. Just before the sun sets, bats pour out from the caves and woods of Consuelo, darkening the sky as they spiral by the thousands to feed on fruits, insects and coconut sap in distant fields.

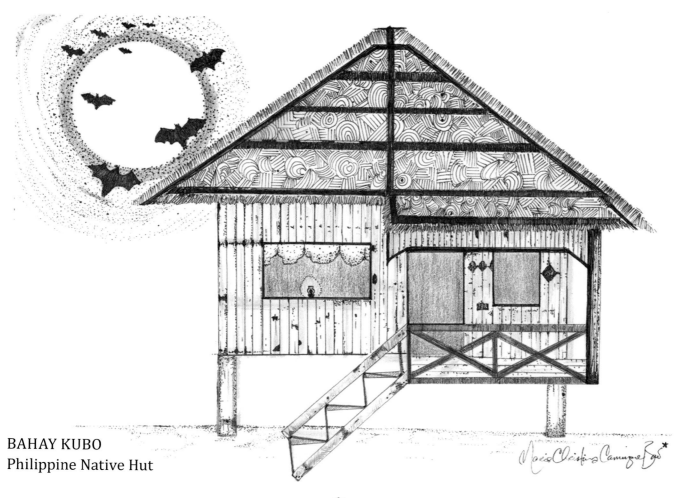

BAHAY KUBO
Philippine Native Hut

The story of Lucita began when her father, Ernesto, *a sayad* or sickle-wielding, *tuba*-gatherer or *mananggite* (toddy collector) found out that the bats were sucking out the *tuba* or coconut sap from the bamboo tubes and containers he left hanging in the coconut trees. He would usually take it down to the village and sell the *tuba* to the hardy men who like to drink strong, fermented coconut wine. The coconut sap is also used to make natural coconut vinegar which is an essential item in every household on the island. The Filipino folks in these rural parts can never do without *tuba*.

But there was nothing to sell now. The bats took away his source of livelihood. He took his slingshot or *tirador* and stormed out of their hut, absolutely fuming. His pregnant wife, Tomasita, was left alone with their six boys at home. Every evening, Ernesto set out into the dark woods and hunted down the culprits - bats. This went on for months until his wife gave birth to a baby girl on November 12.

"What kind of baby is this?" Ernesto, Tomasita's husband, asked, peering into an odd-looking face. Why does she look so ugly?

"Kayaot na wayong!" (She's very ugly!)

Her father was shocked to find a baby with the abnormal features of a bat! Tomasita thought her baby would die because she refused to nurse for two days. Fortunately, on the third day, she finally got her infant breastfeeding normally.

Lucita was not like any other human child. She was born without mammary glands. She had no eyebrows. Her eyes were without lashes, no upper lids, and red-rimmed at the lower lids which were turned outward. She slept with her eyes wide open. There were dark markings on her face, particularly beside her mouth. She had no upper lip. She had little hair on her head. Her tiny ears were only half the size of the ears of any child her age. Her fingers were deformed. The villagers called her *kabog* in the dialect for she had the frightful appearance of a bat.

Lucita was shy and mingled little with kids of her own age. She ran errands for her parents and performed household duties. She washed the family laundry, swept and scrubbed the floor with *walis tingting,* a broom made from natural coconut midribs, and *lampaso,* a fibrous coconut husk used to scrub the wooden floor. She split wood and cooked rice over open wood fire.

In school, she was bullied and the children called her *kabog.* She was visually impaired at birth and because of her defective vision and deformed fingers, she had difficulty learning to read and write. She fell behind in school and had to repeat first grade. She walked down the streets in the village with boys and girls yelping at her heels and making fun of her. She held back the tears until she reached home.

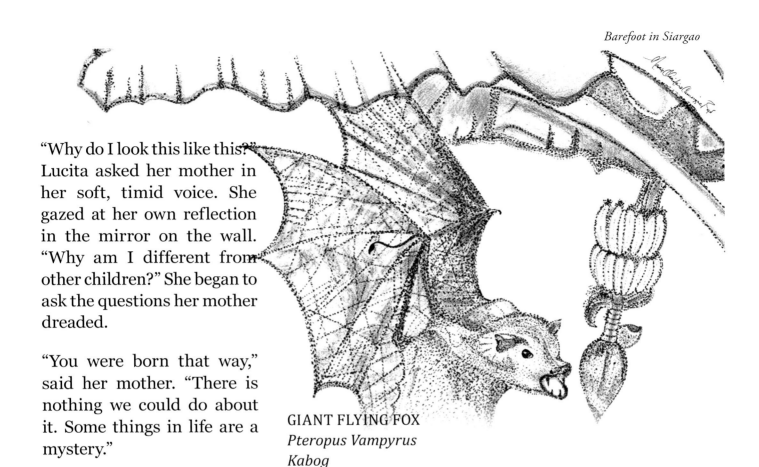

"Why do I look this like this?" Lucita asked her mother in her soft, timid voice. She gazed at her own reflection in the mirror on the wall. "Why am I different from other children?" She began to ask the questions her mother dreaded.

"You were born that way," said her mother. "There is nothing we could do about it. Some things in life are a mystery."

GIANT FLYING FOX
Pteropus Vampyrus
Kabog

Tomasita was ashamed of her daughter's appearance that she couldn't bear to have other people see her. Once, she conceded to her little girl's plea to see the popular surfing event in Cloud Nine. It was Lucita's first time to go and she was very excited because she had heard so much about surfing in Cloud Nine, which was drawing tourists around the world to their small island in the Philippines.

To her dismay, she was left behind in the house of her relatives while they all went out to see the international surfing competition. She never felt so sad and lonely. She felt like an outsider, excluded from enjoying life. But there were some people like Eduvigis, the village midwife, and her husband, Herninio, who treated Lucita like she was one of their own and took her everywhere.

One day in summer, after attending a Catholic mass service at the San Isidro Labrador Chapel or *kapilya,* Lucita went out to play in the street. The sun hurt her eyes so much that it blinded her. Just then, a jeepney came by, speeding along the highway and bumped her. There was a scream and Lucita fell down by the side of the road.

The poor girl was rushed to the Siargao District Hospital in Dapa where she underwent minor suture repair on her hip. The doctors and nurses were also shocked to see somebody who had features resembling those of a bat!

Questions about Lucita's condition compelled the town physician, Dr. Manuel Bauson, to do a physical examination on her and discovered abnormalities in her anatomy. Some doctors say that Lucita's abnormal condition had to do with her mother taking medication or getting sick during the first trimester of her pregnancy.

Soon, a crowd of curiosity-seekers came to see Lucita. Children from the nearby Don Enrique Navarro Memorial School (DENMS) happened along to give Lucita a peep at the hospital. Some even gave cash donations to her family.

*T*he *Freeman Sunday Magazine* in Cebu City ran a story on Lucita and it touched the hearts of the orphans at the Asilo de la Milagrosa who volunteered to give some of their toys and storybooks to her. Another team from *The Freeman Newspaper* was dispatched to Siargao. A newsletter which was circulated around Europe picked up the story and one reader was moved with compassion and reached out and gave financial assistance to her family.

The national media took interest in her and she began appearing in nationwide TV programs. Some foreign tourists even offered to sponsor her plastic surgery but her family was hesitant and afraid. They only gave their consent when the Office of the Vice –President (Noli de Castro), reached out to help their family in 2005 and gave them assurance that the best care will be given to Lucita in surgery. Lucita had a transplant operation at the Philippine General Hospital, where a skin tissue from her own body was grafted into her eyes to form new eyelids. Her mother said the operation was not completed in full because Lucita was eager to go back home to the island to finish high school.

With the aid and support of a generous patron, Rosemarie, a lady dentist who hails from the same town, Lucita was able to study Computer Science at the Advance Institute of Technology in Mactan, Cebu. But she stayed for only two semesters. She left school to find a job and earn her own keep. She moved back to Siargao Island and got a job as a hired help. She went into domestic service and tended small stores to help provide for her family's needs.

The Rufous hornbill, Brahminy kite, Philippine tarsier and giant flying fox find a home in the rolling hills and lush forests of the village of Consuelo.

Lucita, who had learned so much from life and poverty, had in a few years grown confident in her ability to forge her own path in the world. She learned to groom, dress up and take care of herself. She did not spend her time looking over her shoulder and regretting what she did not have. Despite the bullying and prejudice, she overcame difficult odds and found her worth and strength. She even found love. With the kindness and care of some concerned friends, she was able to escape the world of loneliness and isolation, and live her life knowing what it is to love and be loved.

SECRETS OF MY SOUL

Daku Island, General Luna, Siargao Island.

Photo: Faye Monunggolh

Silent woes and happiness
   Lie in my heart
   Restless deep down
Await my soul's caress.

   Laughter is shared
     But tears, concealed
     Clandestine heartaches
Everyone is spared.

My profound love
   Wrapped in secrecy,
   No one knows
But cherubs above.

From God, I have received
   My pleas heeded
   My orisons heard
Oh pure spirit retrieved!

These make me whole....
   The unending depth,
   The deafening silence,
The secrets of my soul.

*Maria Sherrylyn Buo - Sigman

Echoes of Tawin-Tawin Creek

It happened more than 20 years ago, down by the swamp creek of Tawin-Tawin, in the scenic backcountry of General Luna, where lush, green *pijapi, pagatpat, bakhaw*[1] and *nipa*[2] mangroves seem to stretch on from here to eternity. On this particular day in the sunny month of May, the matriarch of the clan, Josefina, joined her son, Fabian or Ben, and her grandchildren, Jopee, Maryrose, Tosh and Den-den, on a trip to the family fish pond in Tawin-Tawin.

BAROTO or BANDUNG
Dug-out canoe

They took off from the *tulay* or bridge and headed upstream in mirror-smooth, dark waters that led all the way to the northern villages of Magsaysay, Catangnan and Cabitoonan. Rising beyond the swamp, away on the other side, gentle rolling hills of brown *Bolinao* soil sloped down into the water. On either side of the swamp, dense thickets of *pijapi, pagatpat, bakhaw* and shrubby *nipa* palms or *kasanihan* stretch endlessly. The tall, shining, smooth leaves of *nipa* are used in shingling the roof of many a rural home in the Philippine countryside.

Kingfisher
Takray

As the motorized pumpboat gets farther and farther off from the Tawin-Tawin Bridge, the wilderness comes to life. The air is filled with the scent of trees and fallen leaves. A splendid kingfisher or *takray*, with a blue head and tail, winged its way overhead and pierced the air with a loud shriek, echoing across the swamp. A black-naped oriole or *kulihaw,* breaks through the twisted branches and hanging roots of the *diakit* or *balete* trees on the hillside. The cawing of the Large-billed crow or *uwak* resonated in the hills beyond. A five-inch baby sailfin lizard or *ibid*, perched on a mangrove tree, is warming itself in the heat of the sun. Another lizard, the monitor or *bibang,* also lurks deep in the mangrove thickets.

PANARES
2015

Philippine Cockatoo
Cacatua haematuropygia
Abucay

This small village used to be the playground of the Philippine cockatoo or *abucay.* In the 1980s, these snow-white landbirds were widespread and commonly seen foraging in the corn fields or *maisan* in the villages of Consuelo and Tawin-Tawin. They can often be seen frequenting the *pagatpat* mangroves where they love to feed on the fruits. The *abucay* is by no means confined to the town of General Luna, thriving in the riverbanks of Del Carmen and in the mountain areas of Sayog, *Barangay* Datu and in Jaboy, Pilar, in the marshlands of San Mateo, Burgos, and in Bancuyo and Bagakay Islands in Dapa. After the deadly Typhoon Nitang[3] hit the Philippines in 1984, the cockatoo population in Siargao Island dwindled alarmingly.

Tawin-Tawin is a mysterious world where a *tambayon*, a medicine man or woman capable of treating both natural and supernatural maladies, seeks the dispensation from spirits to cut down old trees; and sometimes, witches take the shape of large, strange-looking birds that hunt for prey after dark. There is a feeling of solace, mystery and seclusion out here in this realm of mangrove and water. It seems to belong to another time and place, a lonely, forgotten world in which the spirits of the wild come to haunt.

A long time ago, there was a small girl who often went down to the creek to wash her family's clothes. One day, as the hard-working eight-year-old Jerlyn was toiling in the broiling sun on the lonely banks of the stream, beating the dirty clothes hard and clean with a wooden washing paddle or *palo–palo*, there appeared dwarfs or *duwende*[4], tiny men and women, dressed in colorful garb; and they circled charmingly around the rocks, dancing and springing about, and began chattering and laughing but she couldn't make out what they were saying. Jerlyn went pale. Already she felt her hair standing on end from fright. Her skin grew cold. Her heart was beating fast with the shock of this otherworldly and disturbing experience. Her hands trembled so much that she could hardly concentrate on her task. After that, she vowed never to go back to the creek alone again. From then on, she always sought the company of her neighbors whenever she went down to the creek to wash the laundry.

Sometime after the incident, Jerlyn was seized with a sudden, unexplained and protracted illness and she thought she was going to die. The doctors had no rational or medical explanation for her condition. They couldn't do anything to save her so she sought help from Doring, the medicine woman or *tambayon* (folk healer). Miraculously, the age-old healing ritual improved her condition and gradually brought her own healing ability to the surface. She found out she had the hands of a healer and could cure by merely placing her hands on an inflicted person.

* * * * *

A sudden bend in the stream brought the family to an open pond, sparkling and rippling in the summer sun. Sprawling over six hectares, this mosaic of rectangular brackish water ponds are cultivated with *pasayan* (shrimp), *bangus* (milkfish) and *alimango* (mud crab).

The pumpboat docked and they came off in ones and twos. Wasting no time, Jopee and her twelve-year-old cousin, Tosh, ran together and flung themselves into the water, laughing.

"It's very warm," exclaimed Tosh, her big, brown eyes sparkling with excitement.

Everything glittered in the bright cool sunlight. A light breeze stirred the air. At mid-day, the family enjoyed a festive meal of grilled fish, shrimps and steamed crabs, freshly caught from the pond. Afterwards, *Lola* Deding took a *siesta* in the wooden hut, with Nana, the ever-loyal household cook, watching over her while she was sleeping.

Five-year-old Den-den sat down at the edge of the water, dipping her curious fingers in it. Tosh and her cousin, Maryrose, a roly-poly of a girl who loves to have fun, jumped excitedly in the warm, murky waters. The afternoon promised bucolic pleasures and delightful adventures. It was so very quiet that one could hear the birds buzzing and insects humming incessantly.

 **"*H*elp!"**

The cry rang out in the quiet afternoon. Jopee spun around and saw Tosh and Maryrose, flailing and bobbing in the water. She could see Tosh waving an open hand across the distance.

Tosh had lost her balance as she felt the muddy bottom of the pond sag beneath her slippered feet. Both girls had entered a deep section of the pond. The water was already up to their heads and the bottom was slippery. Maryrose, who was heavier than Tosh, reached out and clung to her. Tosh was in danger of being dragged underneath.

"If I am going to die, I will come back and haunt you," Tosh thought grimly as she struggled desperately to loosen the grip of Maryrose, who was panic-stricken and held on to her with both arms because she did not know how to swim.

Tosh was an athlete in school and knew how to swim but first, she needed to break free. She tried kicking her feet but they got buried in the mud. It was difficult staying upright. They had already swallowed mud-water and began gasping for breath.

"Help, help," Tosh cried again.

Jopee heard her screams and in a split-second, she rushed to their side, grabbed Maryrose and pulled her out, setting Tosh free. She then guided Maryrose across the pond and brought her safely ashore. The girls were dreadfully tired and their hands and feet were icy cold as they sat there on the dike.

Their five-year-old cousin, Den-den, saw the whole scene from the cottage and for some

Philippine Sailfin Lizard or *ibid.*

reason, it tickled her funny bone and she started to laugh. She was laughing so hard at her cousins who almost drowned it seemed as if she were being tickled by some invisible little beings. Had she known what was coming next, perhaps she might have been less jubilant.

Later, down at the pond, someone got trapped in deep water, floundering and struggling for a foothold in the slimy bottom.

Tosh was pointing: *"Hala,* Look! Den-den's drowning!"

Sure enough, leaping into the water to save Den-den was Jopee, coming to the rescue for the second time on the same day!

Tosh and Maryrose felt stunned as their rescuer very capably managed to bring Den-den safely to shore and they gaped in amazement as though they could not believe their eyes. How can Jopee be so brave, calm and quick on her feet? Who would have thought their other cousin, like them, would also come close to drowning?

After a shocked silence, Maryrose looked at Tosh and exchanged a sly smile of understanding with her. She giggled. Tosh chuckled, followed by a burst of laughter. For some reason that seemed funny to both of them, they laughed loud and hard until the whole place reverberated with their gay laughter. It looked like they would never stop laughing.

Tawin-Tawin still echoes of their voices and laughter, and that moment in time when a fearless 16-year-old Jopee showed great courage in saving her cousins from drowning.

Christina Camingue Buo

Courage
I shall not be enfeebled
by failures but,
emboldened by GOD

through silence.

*Maria Sherrylyn Buo - Sigman

White-bellied Sea Eagle or *Manauy*.
Del Carmen, Siargao Island.

Photo: Christina Buo

78

A Song in the Wind

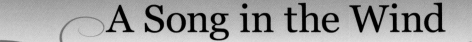

From the open window of the *sala*[1] on the upper floor of the large and airy house, Adrian could see the sky turning purple-pink as dusk fell over the surfing town of General Luna. The ancestral house was close to the beach, where it caught every breeze. Maya birds whistled their last songs of the day among the twilit trees in the garden. The first evening star winked and twinkled down on him.

"May I give you a lift to work?" he asked Aileen, whom he was visiting at her grandparents' home.

"That would be nice. Wait, I'll have to tell *Lola*. I don't want her to worry."

Adrian had offered to take Aileen on his motorbike to the Siargao District Hospital, in the neighboring town of Dapa, where she worked the night shift as a ward nurse.

"*Lola?*" Aileen stepped into the spacious room of her 77-year old grandmother.

"Are you still awake?"

Lola Deding opened her eyes and sat down on the bed. She smiled at her *apo* or grandchild. Aileen was the first daughter of Evelyn, her eldest daughter. She had finished her nursing studies in Cebu and instead of getting a job in big hospitals in the city or out of the country, she chose to work on the remote island to be near to her grandmother and to minister to her needs. *Lola* Deding was just too glad Aileen had come to stay with her in this small town. Life was very lonesome indeed with her adored doctor husband, Pedro or *Indong*, already gone for three years now.

"Yes, I'm just resting."

"Do you want to take your medicine now?"

Grandma nodded as Aileen offered her tablets and a glass of water.

"*Salamat.* You've always taken good care of me."

Then Aileen tucked her into the big, white bed. "Adrian is giving me a ride to Dapa. Good night *Lola*. I'll see you tomorrow."

It was a perfectly clear night in May, and there was a cool wind blowing in softly from the murmuring sea. The fresh, sweet scents and the sounds of a tropical summer evening were all about them. The May moon, round and full, rose above them like a golden goddess in the southeastern sky, bathing the lagoon in loveliness and light.

At eight in the evening, they were riding on the highway on Adrian's Yamaha motorbike, going south to Dapa, the principal town of Siargao Island. From General Luna to Dapa, the road runs at a total distance of 15 kilometers in a southeast-west direction, traversing the rice fields of Tawin-Tawin and Consuelo, past the agricultural areas and grasslands of Osmeña Village. Farther beyond, low hills rose, silhouetted against the purple sky.

Christina Camingue Buo

The village is nodding off to sleep beneath the creeping evening mist. On the outer edge of the town, *nipa* huts become sparse and built up close to the main road. These light, cool, traditional native huts or *bahay kubo* are bounded by mango or other fruit trees and vegetable, herb and flower gardens, with some livestock in the backyard. The full moon shone on wide acres of rice fields and coconut groves and bamboo clumps as they motored down the National highway. They were riding past the *bonak* in Sitio Danao, *Barangay* Osmeña, Dapa, when the motorbike suddenly swerved and skidded out of control. They both tumbled to the ground. Luckily, they were not injured.

All around them lay a strange, dark and desolate marshland. The *bonak* is a seasonal swamp overgrown with wild *carabao* grass, *agsam* ferns, *catmon* and narrow *bangkay*[2] trees, that melted into a range of misty hills, a kilometer distant. These are rolling hills of limestone with the highest point at 128 meters above sea level. In 1990, a 100-hectare Dapa upland reforestation project was undertaken in the area and harvestable species were grown − gmelina[3], mahogany[4] and acacia mangium. *Narra*[5] and *antipolo* trees surround the hills with *sajapo, buyakan* and exotic fruit trees such as *marang, langka* and *lanzones.*

One time, Aileen's *Tia* Romana and her husband, *Tio* Rodelio were traveling to Dapa in the wee hours to catch the early morning boat trip to Surigao City when they saw a civet cat or *katujo* leap down the road in front of their vehicle and disappeared into the swamp.

This seasonal wetland dries up in the hot summer but overflows during heavy monsoon rains, lasting for weeks or even months. When the area is inundated, locals ride a *baroto*[6] or *gakit*, a raft made of banana trunks, to cross to the other side.

Shadows on a Lonely Highway
Christina Buo, 2015.

The scenic highway which links the principal town of Dapa to General Luna and other towns of Siargao runs past the bonak, a habitat for endemic species of plants, trees, birds and animals.

Christina Bu

Aileen felt as if she and Adrian were the only persons on earth. It was as if they were carried away in a dream to another world, a night-corner of the earth, vast, silent and secret. There was no house in sight. There was no one around; no man, woman, child, or anything, to break the silence and stillness of the night. On the left side, a massive rock gleamed in the moonlight and cast sinister black shadows. It had a haunting presence by night.

What was that?

Something was in the air that night. She heard a strange voice of a woman, borne on the wind, singing very close behind her just before the motorbike went crashing near the queer-shaped monolith on the roadside. She shivered and crossed her arms over her chest. She kept silent and stood next to Adrian, who was doing a quick, cursory examination of his motorbike to find out what went wrong.

There it goes again.

Out of the silence came the sound of a woman's voice singing a melancholy song. It sounded like the sad notes of a Tagalog love song heard long ago. Aileen goes gooseflesh all over. Her heart beat faster and faster. She closed her eyes and held her breath.

It was audible indeed and a hard one to mistake. She heard a woman's voice which was very clear in this solitary spot. The voice sounded on, piercing the heart with its beauty and melancholy; it drifted over them like haunted music the wind blows across a dark, lonely countryside on a moonlit night. After some time it became faint and then the singing waned and wavered into the silence of the summer night.

Awooh... awooh ... awooh ...

In the distance, a dog began to howl mournfully, under the mystical full moon. Soon as they heard it, the engine starts. "Stroke of luck," Adrian thought to himself as he managed to start the engine and continued on their way.

Next day, Aileen questions Adrian when he came by her grandparents' house again to visit.

"Who was that woman singing last night?" was her first query.

"Woman? What woman?"

"I heard a woman singing just before we crashed. It sounded like she was very close behind me."

"I didn't hear a woman singing last night. How can that possibly be? That place is deserted. Nobody lives out there."

Diving into Happiness.
Camaligan, Dapa
Siargao Island.

Photo: Christina Buo

Christina Camingue Buo

Christina's World, Manuel Pañares, 2015.

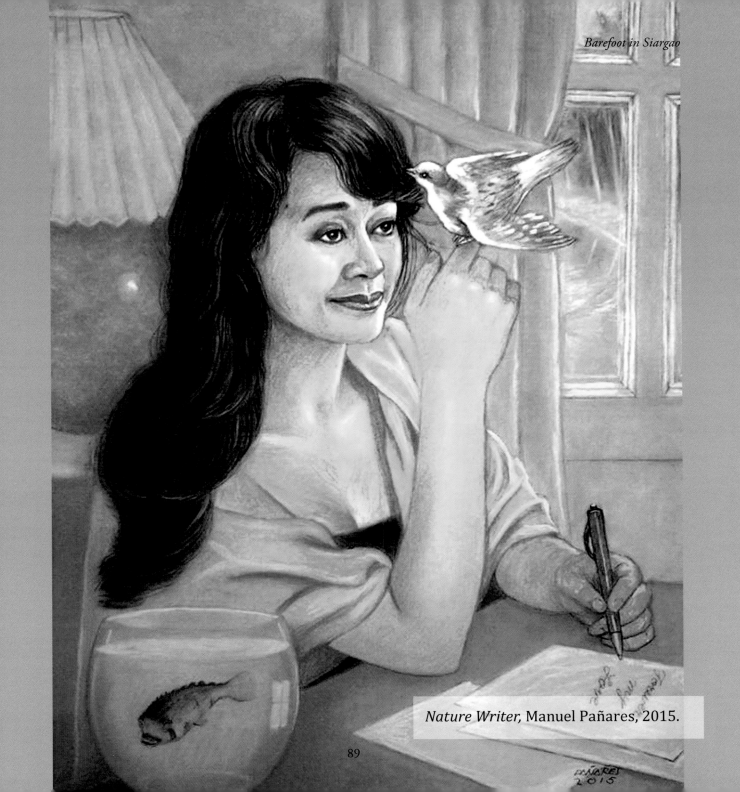

Nature Writer, Manuel Pañares, 2015.

Christina Caminguel...

Mariang Makiling, Manuel Pañares, 2015.

Summer of Lilies, Manuel Pañares, 2018.

Christina Camingue Buo

Lady in Blue, Manuel Pañares, 2015.

My Prayer, Manuel Pañares, 2015.

Sunset Enchantment, Manuel Pañares, 2015.

See the World Anew, Manuel Pañares, 2015.

The Medicine Woman

A Tribute to the *Manhilot* or *Albularyo*

I could only grimace in pain as I tripped and tumbled on the ground during a soccer match between us, city girls and the country boys, on a sweltering May afternoon in the playground of the General Luna Central Elementary School in Siargao Island.

My 9-year-old cousin, Yves Martini, darted across the field and knelt beside me.

"Are you all right?"

"I think I broke my ankle," I told him.

It hurt so much I could not walk on it and after a while, I realized this was the last time I would play soccer. My right foot was limp and so sore that I had to take off my running shoes, after running for hours on the grass.

Early in the afternoon, we, the *bakasyonista*[1] girls from the city, challenged several high school boys in town to a game of soccer - baseball. It was our childhood game and we still haven't grown out of it yet. We felt that we could take on the boys and beat them. Call it the arrogance of youth but we had our share of athletic talents in the family.

There was my sporty sister, Tosh, and my athletic cousin, Jopee, who both played for the all-girls soccer - baseball teams at Saint Theresa's College in Cebu City. Tosh and Jopee were the tomboys in the clan and both were very clever at all sports. Jopee competed in softball and volleyball in the Cebu City National Science High School and she also qualified to participate in the Regional Sports Meet. She also played for the University of San Carlos – College of Engineering Women's Soccer-Baseball Team. With these strong and fast girls on our team, how can we possibly lose?

The game was running at fever-pitch, the crowd was getting bigger and our team was leading by several points, when I lost my footing while sprinting to third base, and sprained my ankle.

The game ended abruptly; the crowd of youngsters dispersed; and I was limping back towards my grandparents' house assisted by family and friends.

I met my Uncle Ben on my way up the stairs and he saw my swollen foot.

"That's what happens when you get careless," he said as he passed me on the stairway.

"At least we won the game," I consoled myself.

If my grandfather, *Lolo Indong*, were alive today, he would have taken me to his medical clinic at the ground floor of the ancestral house and gently treated my foot injury, without censure or rebuke.

After dinner, it was decided that I should be taken to the home of the local *manhilot*[2] or herb healer, who employs chiropractic massage and uses leaves, herbs, and roots to cure the sick. She is also reputed to have special or spiritual powers that can treat supernatural maladies.

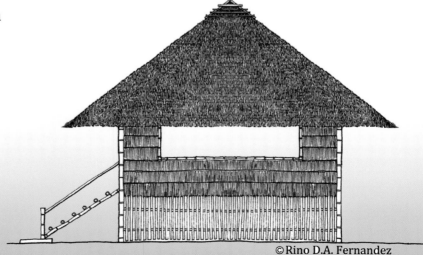

©Rino D.A. Fernandez

Eleonora Valerio, known as *Manang*[3] Doring, was an old widow who lived in a tiny *bahay kubo*[4] at the back of the *kumbento* or convent of the Santo Tomas de Villanueva Parish Church in *Purok* 3[5]. She was the *tambayon, mananambal* or shaman of our town. The local folks turned to her for physical and spiritual healing remedies. She knew all the plants, flowers and trees that make good medicine. For those who were "possessed" or afflicted with supernatural diseases, she performed traditional, revered rituals and offered prayers for treatment. As a medicine woman, she served as an intermediary between mystical entities and human beings. She was a cosmic warrior who engaged in combat with invisible foes in the spirit world.

Special folks like *Manang* Doring possessed the knowledge of medicinal herbs and plants and learned to use what nature provided for medicine. In the old days in the Philippines, there were very few doctors in the rural areas and people went to the medicine man or woman for help when they got sick. My childhood friend, Gay, whose family lives next door to *Manang* Doring, the medicine woman, says she has known her since she was ten. Her mother, Gracia, a school principal, and her brothers and sisters would come running to her when they are ill, tired or weak. Some folks seek her for remedies for bruises, wounds and various illnesses - fever, head and stomach pain, colds and cough, allergies, rheumatism and diarrhea.

For fever, *Manang* Doring prescribed herbal drinks made from the bark and roots of trees that have been cut down by the slash-and-burn *kaingin* farming. For flatulence or fractures and sprains, she uses *tuba-tuba* leaves smeared with oil and warmed over a flame then wrapped around the affected part on the body. She also boiled tea from the roots and leaves of the *tuba-tuba* to treat diarrhea. She pounded and used *sagbong* or *sambong* leaves as a cure for headache. The decoction of *sambong* leaves and roots were also used to relieve stomach ache and cure fever.

She roamed the forest in Bayud and wandered through coconut groves along the shore, harvesting specimens of wild herb shrubs and roots, which are mixed with her homemade *lana* or virgin coconut oil. If she's not able to make her own *lana*, she uses the holy oil consecrated for healing from the parish. The Blessing of oil takes place on Holy Wednesday or *Miyerkules Santo* during the Holy Week (*Semana Santa)* observance in the Catholic Church.

My friend, Baning, helped me as I hobbled down the dark road until we came upon a little hut, where a faint light glowed through the half-open window.

"*Buenas. Maayong gabii. Jaoy tawo?* Good evening. Is anybody home? Baning called out.

An old woman, barefoot, shriveled up and bent with age, carrying a *lamparilla* or a small glass oil lamp, opened the door and asked us to come inside. My sisters, cousins and other friends waited outside, beneath the lamp post in a corner of the street.

The hut was bare of furnishings and we sat there in the middle of the wooden floor where the *manhilot* rubbed my right leg with thick coconut oil and applied the *hilot* massage on my swollen ankle. She was a small woman with a wrinkled face, dark eyes and long, abundant white hair, in tangles. In the subdued light, she seemed like a strange phantom vision in her white garment. She seemed old but wise and strong.

GUAVA
Psidium guajava
Bayabas

"You have dislocated a bone in your ankle and I'm going to reset it," she told me.

How I groaned! It hurt! I tried not to cry in pain. I did not want my friend, Baning, to think I'm a cry baby at 21! My strength gave out and I thought I would faint after the *hilot*. The leaves of the *bayabas* or guava were applied on my sprained ankle, which served both as medicine and bandage.

"Change the guava leaves dressing every day until the swelling goes down," *Manang* Doring advised me.

I nodded a yes.

It did its job well and in two weeks, the pain in my ankle gradually subsided and I could walk again. I regained full strength and stamina in a short time. No crutches, no sprained ankle plaster cast, no orthopedic surgery, just the age-old miracle art of *hilot* therapy using bare hands and herbs.

Manang Doring, the medicine woman, was a master of the art of healing. She embraced the wisdom of old, gathered the providence of nature and kept alive the ancient way of healing in the Filipino culture. Whether it was handed down to her by her own folks or self-study, I do not know. I only know that her gift saved the lives of many and made me walk again.

Love exhilarates
as much as it exasperates.
Burns as much as it freezes
Comforts as much as it hurts
Lingers as much as it fades
It is too much of a contradiction,
that only the pure-hearted
can endure beyond forever.

* Maria Sherrylyn Buo - Sigman

Blooming Water Lily.
Sta. Monica, Siargao Island.

Photo: Christina Buo

Christina Camingue Buo

Christmas in Anajawan

It was the eve of Christmas, cold and wet, several years ago, and I was sitting on an empty beach, at a quarter to nine, in the remote island of Anajawan (Ana-ha'wan). The stars twinkled, and lightning quivered about the vast horizon. Then out of the darkness a strange light, as of a globe of fire, appeared above the water. It was unlike anything I had ever seen and I was mystified by it.

Winds of Siargao, Manuel Pañares, 2015.

I had always wished to spend more time in Anajawan, which holds a fascination of the mysterious for me. Located eight nautical miles off General Luna in Siargao, it is the town's farthest outlying island *barangay*. The island is ringed by blue seas, abounding in marlin, *isda sa bato*[1], *nokus*, *lunga*[2] and *tambuli*[3] shells. I went there for the first time in 1999 on an island-hopping excursion with my high school friend, Faye, and my cousin, Mateo. I was back again in the island on a charity mission in July 2005, with my youngest sister, Mashelle.

It is sunny and dry from May to September but the northeast monsoon or *amihan*, which occurs from November to February, brings huge waves and heavy rain[4]. This is of great concern to the *tuba*-gatherers[5], fisherfolk and all the people of Anajawan because they rely on fishing and copra for their livelihood and sustenance. When there is a shortage or scarcity of fish, they cross over miles and miles of water just to buy rice and other basic needs in the mainland. Food and travel become a serious problem in the out-of-the-way islands like Anajawan, La Januza, Suyangan, and Mam-on.

Dwarf Sperm Whale (mother and calf)
Kogia sima

"Are you really going?" asked my Aunt Camila, sounding worried and incredulous over the phone. She and my Uncle Lalo were in Cebu for the holidays while I was in town planning my upcoming birthday and Christmas adventure in Anajawan Island.

"Yes," I said, Could you spare some old clothes? The fishermen and their families in the island might like to have them."

"Go down to the stockroom," she told me, "and take all the clothes you want. If you need more food to take with you, there's meat in the freezer, some crabs, and see if you can find pasta for spaghetti in the *aparador*."[6]

"Thank you, *Mama* Mila," I answered, and went excitedly down to the stockroom. There were all sorts of coats, sweaters, cardigans, men's shirts, women's blouses, dresses and long pants hanging in the racks.

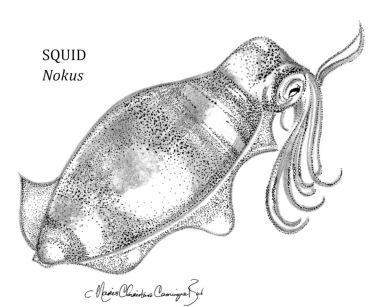

SQUID
Nokus

"Why don't you just give out these things there in the town?" she asked. "Do you really have to travel that far? I heard it's been raining non-stop. It will be difficult to travel to the islands."

I might have answered her a hundred reasons. I had resolved to celebrate every birthday in a unique way, out there exploring a new place, meeting the local folks, listening to their stories, gift-giving and sharing blessings. Instead, I simply said to her, "Because I want to."

December 24 dawned radiant over the eastern border of Siargao Island, and the sun, sea, and sky was all blue and golden that morning. It was a quarter past eight o'clock and I stood on the wharf with my nine-year-old companion, Bulutong, waiting for Corio, our boatman, to arrive from Anajawan Island. The charter boats and fishing vessels bobbed up and down the water and one middle-aged man, seated in the stern, bailed out seawater from the bottom of a small pumpboat. Ten minutes later, a cyan-colored boat approached the wharf landing and a bronze-skinned fisherman, with a cone-shaped *sarok*[7] hat on his head, climbed out and headed in our direction.

At last Corio arrived and we loaded our containers of boiled rice and freshly-cooked food, luggage, and sacks of clothes one after the other onto the bottom planks of the boat. There were only three of us on this trip. The sky was perfectly clear and a cool breeze blew my hair back from my face as we plowed our way across the blue-green waters of the lagoon, silvered with sunlight. I was happy God answered my prayer for fine weather on this journey.

The trip to Anajawan afforded us breathtaking views of stunning emerald islands overhung with coco palms. Sometimes, the wind kicks up heavy seas and we would coast in on the crest of a huge wave; the sprightly winds sending spray, keeping us cool in the sun. I particularly enjoyed the drama of the islands fringed by sugar-fine, white sands, and sparkling blue-green water. The waves off Daku Island are fluid walls of glass and sometimes, you see surfers ride its picturesque breaks. *Tayos* or flying fish glide past us and *bayo* (needlefish) hurled themselves out of the water; a venomous sea snake[8] or *dayag asaw,* banded with brilliant green and black stripes, twisted and floated up to the water's surface.

We covered the distance to Anajawan in almost two hours. At a quarter to ten, we landed on the shore. There were families, mothers holding crying babies, children clinging to their mother's skirts, laughing and playing, their dark eyes shining, mouths gaping. I even spotted a familiar smiling face - that of my cousin, Yves Martin's former nanny or *yaya* Lina, carrying her infant.

A young man in yellow jersey was playing beautiful music with his guitar and girls and boys were singing along with him. Corio called out to his wife, Lyden, waiting by the boats, full of smiles and enthusiasm. Then we unloaded our goods and I followed her home while Corio and the men hauled up the pumpboat.

Everyone was invited to join me in the cabana for my birthday beach picnic, and with candles in hand, the villagers regaled me with traditional Surigaonon[9] songs and offered me bouquets of pink roses, *santan,* hibiscus and bougainvillea, handpicked from their gardens. There was plenty of food such as *adobong baboy*[10], *alimango* (crab), spaghetti and sweet glutinous rice or *biko* which Boday, our 19-year-old household cook, prepared the day before. We sang and danced, and laughed and made merry.

In the afternoon, Bulotong and I walked down to the other end of the island and turned in at the huts of the *mananagat* or fishermen, and distributed clothes and school supplies.

"Are you selling them?" asked a fisherman.

I told them no, much to their shocked delight. In a small *nipa* hut by the beach, one fisherman sat in a semi-circle with his five small children on the wooden floor. A small pot of rice was boiling over burning wood in their *abuhan*[11].

"We thank God we have something to eat this Christmas," he told me with a smile. "It's difficult to catch fish these days."

I stayed in the home of Macedonio Espiel, a village official. He and his wife, Lilia Forcadilla, were full of kindness and generosity. They showed me the kind of hospitality Filipinos are known the world over. There in a house overlooking the sea, I stayed in the room vacated by the village schoolteacher, Melanie, my childhood friend, who returned to her family in *Purok* 2 in the *poblacion* for the holidays.

In the night, the rain fell heavily and I stayed indoors, watching my host, *Manang* Lilia, cook *biko na linunokan*[12] over a wood fire. Her husband, *Manoy*[13] Cedo, split wood and threw them into the fire.

When the rain subsided at half past eight, I decided to go out for a walk on the beach. Bulutong had already fallen asleep so I asked a local boy, nine-year-old Nickver, who had been trailing us the whole afternoon, to come along with me. We passed under solar-powered lamp posts which illuminated the sandy streets. For a population of about 500 people, only very few can afford electricity or solar-powered electric supply in the island. When we came out to the beach, it was dark and deserted. There were no boats out at sea. Nothing disturbed the absolute stillness of the place.

I could just sit here on the sand and be lulled by the peace and quiet. Nickver started digging in the sand.

"I found one," he muttered, *"karaykay."* I smiled; ghost crabs are my friends.

Great bolts of lightning flashed across the dark horizon. Suddenly out in the blackness, I heard a sound, a faint splash in the water. I looked to my right and perceived what seemed to be a figure of a man with his arms coming out of the water. Then I saw a sight as strange – a phosphorescent ball of light lay over the surface of the water, maybe no more than 20 meters away from where we sat. The light intensified, and after a moment went out. It reappeared on the same spot and then, vanished again. It came out of the night, glowing with a fiery, unnatural luster, but did not shed light around. It had no reflection on the water; it didn't move from its place. *What can it be?*

I refused to believe it was anything supernatural. But I couldn't explain what occurred before my very eyes. I've just seen something which did not seem reasonable to my understanding. I couldn't dismiss what I saw as just a figment of my imagination. Suddenly my heart started pounding and I began experiencing a creepy, unnerving sensation all over my body. Never had I felt so frightened!

"Let's go!" I blurted out. On impulse, we turned and bolted down the street. When we finally reached the house, we told *Manoy* Cedo about the apparition.

"You've just seen a *santelmo*,[14]" he said it so simply that it's hard not to accept it as a matter of fact. "Is it raining?"

"Yes, it is drizzling," I replied.

'They usually come out in the evening when it's slightly raining."

Manoy Cedo recounted a tragic incident during the *fiesta*[15] a year ago when a drunken man slipped out of the boat that was supposed to take him back home to the neighboring island of La Januza, fell into the water and then died on the spot. *Was there a connection between his death and the strange occurrence?* Folks around these parts believe that these flaming masses of light are ghostly forms of lost souls.

I have heard sightings of a gleaming body of flame that roll and undulate, swirling and spouting forth into the cold night air, like what locals call *santelmo* or Saint Elmo's fire. There have been similar incidents reported by locals and relevant sightings by people I know.

In the early 1980s when there was still no electricity in Siargao, twelve-year-old Jerlyn and her friend were out in a dark road in the village of Malinao, waiting for their classmate when they saw a light flickering down the road some distance away. Thinking it was her friend Jerlyn advanced towards it and began scolding her, "Where have you been? What took you so long? We have been waiting for you for hours!"

To her utter amazement, it was not her friend she saw but this smoldering flame zigzagging in the darkness, in blue, yellow, orange and red colors, exploding like fireworks! Strangely, the thing seemed to respond to being shouted at. Terror gripped her and she began to run. Her friend got a glimpse of it and ran, too. Jerlyn was a slow runner compared to her athlete friend who could run like a deer. She fought her way through the pitch-black darkness and she ran as hard as she could run, and never stopped until she found a hut in the woods.

Once inside, she saw a kind-faced, elderly couple sitting at the table; the tiny flame of an oil lamp cast a dim circle of light around them. Up the stairs, she climbed, panting and out of breath, and afterward, she stumbled and fell. When she came round, she was alone. She turned and looked at her surroundings but to her astonishment, the house had vanished.

"Jerlyn! Jerlyn! Jerlyn! Where are you?"

She heard her friends calling out to her and they were surprised to find her lying on the grass. Here in this spot where she sought shelter at the home of kind strangers, she saw nothing but trees.

"I believe the old man and his wife were angels sent by God to protect me," she said to her friends as she recounted the incident.

Jess, a 25-year old security guard, who works at a beach resort in Bucas Grande, told me about an incandescent object that appeared at a distance, while he was out walking one moonless night in his hometown in Surigao del Sur.

"There was a glare and it seemed to grow, quite slowly, as it moved towards me. I knew what it was but I wasn't afraid. I took a *posporo* from my pocket and struck the match six or seven times. And then, the *santelmo* suddenly disappeared. It drove it away. "

My own experience was just as frightening and defies reason. No one can feel the fear unless he has seen the phenomenon. How can I explain the unreasoning terror and effect it had upon those of us who beheld it?

After overcoming my initial shock and fright, I wandered to the beach the next morning. I took a small bottle of holy oil, which was blessed by my friend, Fr. Abundio of the Salesians of Don Bosco (SDB), made the sign of the cross, poured drops of holy oil on the sand and prayed for that man and the lost souls.

The strange phenomenon is one of the great mysteries of the island and it recurs, time and again, in solitary places when the night is at its **darkest.**

THIS GREAT LITTLE SOUL

The cerulean sky astounds
glistening stars dazzle
and the beautiful moon beguiles
a great little soul
that fights life's evil

and holds on to God's will.

The cerulean sky astounds
glistening stars dazzle
and the beautiful moon beguiles
a great little soul
that drifts through life's murk
and strives for dreams' truth.

This complex world confounds
cruel ones deject
and the dreary time saddens
a poor little soul
that clings to life's hope
and prays for God's weal.

The dirty mind warns
sultry pluck tempts
and the worldly heart pules
a poor little soul
that lives in life's light
and thrives on earth's purge.

* Maria Sherrylyn Buo – Sigman

Tigasao Cave Lagoon,
San Isidro, Siargao Island

Photo: Dennis Dulguime

Who Hitch-hikes in the Highway?

Beep! Beep!

My Uncle Lalo pressed the horn of his sleek, garnet-red Isuzu D-MAX for no apparent reason as we drove past the rural village of Osmeña, along the National highway. My Aunt Camila sat in the front seat, while my mother, Evelyn, my aunt, Marilyn, and I, piled into the back. We had just flown to Siargao Island from Cebu and it was almost noon by the time my uncle whisked us away from the Sayak Airport in Del Carmen, onto the high road through the open country, like he had wings to fly.

"I blow my horn every time I pass this way," he told us.   I'm not superstitious but I will tell you something that happened to me a long time ago."

"Have you seen ghosts?"I asked him.

"I keep an open mind on the possibility of their existence. That incident taught me to show respect to the invisible entities or what we call *dili ingon nato*[1]..."

Thus he began his story.

Stars in the Sky, Christina C. Buo, 2015.

Photo by Christina Buo

I had traveled over this old highway since I was 17. It usually took about 30-45 minutes to get to Dapa from General Luna over what had been a very rough, rugged country road back then. But I could get there half the time. *Mama* had warned me of my fast and furious driving. I was young, restless and fearless. I loved the sensation of speeding across the country on my father's open jeep.

In the early years of my marriage, I would often travel around the island for my "traveling show" with my *barkada* or buddies. I rented a film projector from Pat's Radio Shop in Surigao City and we would travel to all the towns in Siargao Island, showing Hollywood movies as well as Tagalog films featuring the popular Filipino action hero, Fernando Poe, Jr.

We kept our equipment in the *bodega* or storage room of the house of my *lumon* or relative, then Dapa Mayor Blas Cervantes. We usually start the show at 7 pm or later, as soon as we were able to fill the hall with spectators. And it was usually midnight when we would come back home. I am accustomed to driving on the dark highway at night. In the 1960s, there was no electricity yet in Siargao Island.

We started out for Dapa as it was growing dark. But I could still see the shady groves, green hill slopes and rice paddies in the fading light. I drove on and on without seeing another human being on the road. As we were passing by Malinao crossing, I suddenly felt a hard smack on the left side of my body. *Ugh!* It was as if a needle pierced my shoulder and a sharp searing pain burned in my cheek. I cannot explain what or who hit me; my face and shoulder were struck violently as if by mighty invisible sharp claws.

Soon as we reached Dapa, I went to see my cousin, Dr. Aida Cervantes, the town's very first (woman) doctor. She told me in an offhand diagnosis that I looked all right and she didn't find marks upon my face. The pain persisted though, which meant that I had not been hallucinating.

That night I had a dream and I saw a horrible, black, hairy, ugly giant *Agta[2] or Kapre[3]* glaring down at me! The creature stamped both feet upon the ground and threw up its large hairy hands as if to frighten me. But I wasn't the man to be intimidated by anyone if I could help it.

So I wrestled with the hideous monster. I cannot say how long it lasted. *Thud!* Then I I heard a falling object and woke up to find my wife, Camila, lying on the floor and our bed in a terrible mess, evidence of my struggle with the dark creature that appeared in my nightmare.

I am convinced that there is an invisible realm that exists beyond our ordinary senses. Their inhabitants wander all over the face of the earth and sometimes become visible to us. Some of us see them, some of us don't. But we need not be afraid. God is our power and shield.

* * * * *

Another strange experience happened to me when I was invited to a noontime *salo-salo*[4] at the home of my *saop* or tenant, Tomas, during the fiesta celebration in the small village of Osmeña in Dapa. I drove for miles and miles along the highway at high noon. Up the main road to where a dirt track in the woods leads to *Sitio* Bingag on the left and turning east to the house of Tomas where a native citrus tree or *suwa* grew by the wayside. His *nipa* hut stood fifty meters off the right side of the highway. My companions proceeded ahead of me. Just as I was climbing the steps leading to the entrance door, a group of women

Suwa
Native Citrus Fruit

and young girls suddenly joined me and together we walked up the wooden *hagdan* or stairway.

"You see, Lalo, we have been trying to hitch a ride with you but you never give us a lift," an old woman said.

I got a strange sort of shock at this opening conversation. I looked at them as we reached the balcony. We seated ourselves on the wooden benches. There were five or six of them – young girls, ladies and old women, none of whom I recognize as having seen before. They looked ordinary and wore white clothes.

"But I have never seen you on the road," I answered.

"We have flagged you down so many times on the highway but you just pass us by," said another woman.

The women stated their plea earnestly, their eyes solemn.

"When? How long ago?" I asked them. "How can I let you ride with me when I have never even seen you, waving your hands at me on the road?"

"You never let us ride with you," she stated.

"Why have you never shown yourselves to me? If I had only seen you on the highway, I would surely give you a lift."

The women never shifted their gaze away from me. Their faces were very still; they simply stared at me quietly.

"*Mangajo ra kan ako nan dispensa.* I'm sorry I owe you an apology. Next time, I'll honk the horn and let you ride with me," I assured them.

I looked inside the house and saw Tomas waiting for me in the *sala* where he laid out *lechon*[5], *kalderetang kanding* or goat stew, and *kalibre* (cassava or *balanghoy*) in the dining table, complete with *kinilaw*[6] and *tuba* or palm toddy.

"Why don't we go inside and have something to eat?"

I had scarcely finished asking my question when I turned to see all of them gone, in the twinkling of an eye. *Where did they go?*

"Have you seen the women and children I was talking to just now?" I asked Tomas.

"I didn't see anyone but you in the balcony," he replied. "I thought it rather strange to see you talking to no one but yourself."

Nobody had seen the women and children I met that day. They simply vanished without a warning and I have never seen them again.

Pacific waves peel endlessly into the beautiful beach of Pacifico in the northern coastal town of San Isidro, Siargao Island.

Photo: Dennis Dulguime

A Walk in the Woods

Alfredo lived with his family in a small clearing at the edge of the forest, all shut off from the rest of the world. He worked on the land that belonged to a well-to-do family in the village. He planted *kalibre* (cassava) and *camote* (sweet potato) crops and raised chickens. He climbed coconut trees and gathered *tuba*; he harvested the ripe nuts, scraped off the kernels, laid them out to dry in a *tapahan*[1] and sold the copra to the folks in town.

He was a man who had a direct knowledge of the land, weather and all plant and animal life. He knew the movements of the winds and can smell rain from afar. He knew the forest and its inhabitants. He could tell a creature by the footprints it left on the ground. He was as much a part of the forest as the birds and the trees.

Hoot, hoot. Owls whistled far away over a grove. The cries of the *kalaw* or Rufous hornbills echo among the hills. A Brahminy kite glides overhead and wings home to roost in the *lauaan* tree. Black-naped orioles and the elusive emerald pigeon or *bayud*, with emerald green plumage, feed on the fruits off the *diakit*[2] tree. Asian koels (*bahaw*), coleto (*sungko-langit*), starlings (*lansijang*) and fruit doves (*alimukon*) mingle with the winds in the branches and make music like harmonies made in heaven.

In the woods where tiny squirrels (*buot*) rippled along leafy boughs and civet cats *(katujo)* prowl around, Alfredo wandered down to the rocky crevices and dark caverns. Reticulated pythons (*amamaton*) were there, as thick as a man's thigh and as long as a row of six bicycles, crawling and crushing their prey by constriction.

Civet Cat
Katujo

There came large hooded snakes such as the spectacled cobra, with its poisonous fangs, creeping on the forest floor. Here lay in wait, the subtle *lukay-lukay* snake, which takes the shape and color of a green branch and hang from a guava tree, and so pounce on the unsuspecting tree frog.

The elusive tarsiers[3], owl-eyed and nimble-footed, leap from tree to tree; they trip up and down the *bayagon* and swing on the dangling vines. While he was hacking away at the underbrush with his *sundang* or *buyo* knife, he found a tiny tarsier suckling her offspring under the leafy shade of the *minonga* tree.

Once, Alfredo found a civet pup out in the mountains, lying alone in the cogon grass, wailing and quivering in the heavy rain. He picked it up and brought it home. He and his wife, Sofronia or Ponyang, nursed the civet kitten and let it loose when it was big enough to venture on its own.

Philippine Tarsier
Tarsius syrichta
Amag

The sun begins to set and far away in the marshes, the golden-crowned fruit bats[4] nesting on the *lanipaw* trees awake and make high squeaky sounds as they set forth at dusk. On the ground below, bat droppings accumulate and turn into guano, fertilizing the soil and infecting the air with its rank and pungent odor. From the dark caves, hundreds and hundreds of bats pour out in tight formation, like a big, black cloud spinning across the sky, bound for their favorite hunt.

Night had fallen completely. The full moon topped the trees and cast a ghostly path; witching shadows vanished round corners. The air was buzzing with crickets. Alfredo was returning home to his hut in the woods. In his waist, he carried a *buyo* or a *bolo* knife. The way got darker as he walked on.

Philippine National Animal
Carabao or *Kabaw*

And then, he became aware of something dark coming towards him. In the pale moonlight he saw it, a *carabao* or water buffalo, crouching under the shadows, not more than 15 feet from him and staring at him contemptuously, his nostrils dilated. Its blazing red eyes, flickering like fire, gleamed at him through the dark with fierce menace. He knew then that the creature meant to attack him.

It was evident to him at once that this was no ordinary animal. Of course he knows that *carabaos* are pastured in a *sagbutan,* or grazing land, and tied to a tree, during the night. Real ones don't roam the woods at night attacking people.

The next moment, it lunged at him. Quickly, he seized his *sundang* from its sheath and struck across the back of the savage beast. Another swift blow and the brute began to halt in its career. Weaker and weaker it became, as it reeled under the sharp blows. To Alfredo, there was no terror of the dark, no fear of the wild, no horror of *aswang*[5].

When at last, bleeding and weakened, the *carabao* staggered on its feet. Later, he was astonished to find that it had changed into a human being! He recognized the man from the town. Naked from the waist up, the man still bore the wounds on his body as he retreated into the darkness. He died two months later.

One evening in November, Alfredo, his wife, Ponyang, and their youngest child were walking towards their humble home in the forest when they ran into a baby boy who sprang up suddenly along the path. He brushed aside their little daughter.Ponyang reacted with horror when she saw this little naked boy, as dark as the night. "Who are you?" There was no reply. Instead, the small boy clutched Alfredo's thigh and then, fled into the woods. When he woke up in the morning, Alfredo found blood on his big toe. He had suspected it was a *tianak*[6], a baby who died before it was baptized, and became a lost spirit. Anyone who follows it will get lost.

The silence in the forest is profound, broken only by the occasional songs of birds. Nights are mysterious, pulsing with something unknown. There in the dappled shadows of the trees, invisible eyes are watching and waiting.

Black-naped oriole
Kulihaw

129

For men like Alfredo, the land is their school of life. It is the repository of traditional knowledge and folklore.

In his humble *nipa* hut, Alfredo was awakened in the middle of the night from his sleep by the sound of scratching ... *scratch, scratch, scratch.* He rose from the *baliu banig,* a handwoven sleeping-mat, seized his flashlight and air gun. He rushed to the *abuhan* (kitchen) where he saw a light-brown rat, bigger than normal, scurrying among the pots and pans. With a single shot from his air gun, he hit it in the feet and it disappeared.

As he stared out the window, an *aswang* appeared in the front yard, her malevolent eyes fixed on him. The moon passed between the clouds and shone through a space of trees, illumining the diabolical creature in front of him. Never had he seen anything so hideous. Her long black hair stood on end; her face was wrinkled; her cheeks were hollow; her eyes were wild.

On impulse, he fired one shot at the *aswang* or witch and made a resounding hit on the chest, with the marble ball. After firing two more volleys, it backed off and turned away, limping into the shadows. He realized it was the witch that had entered his hut in the form of a rat[7]. Later, he learned that the woman became paralyzed and cannot walk again.

Out of the hush and stillness of the forest, deadly animals hunt, terrible creatures lurk and otherworldly beings wander. The wind whispers something in his ears and shadows come sweeping after him at dusk. Alfredo has a feeling he is being followed but he walks on, with a brave heart, into the wild woods.

Philippine Grass Owl
Kumotkot

Beyond in Siargao

The small village of Bagakay in Dapa is an example of local folks living in harmony with the environment, planting and growing mangroves, which serves as a habitat for birds, fishes and other marine life, land-builder and buffer zone from calamities.

Christina Camingue Buo

Journey into the Wild

There is a hushed feeling of breathless awe as we crossed the threshold of Sohoton Cave in Bucas Grande[1], part of the Siargao Islands Protected Landscapes and Seascapes[2]. A moment later, effulgent sunlight flooded the passage and we emerged into an enchanting emerald lagoon, open to the sky but otherwise enclosed by limestone rock formations and mushroom-shaped islands.

The September sun poured its radiance and everything seemed to glow as we paddled our kayaks across the blue lagoon in Sohoton. It was as if we entered a sacred and secret water garden of Eden, throbbing with beauty, wonder, and mystery. We drifted near forested islands where the ironwood or *mangkono*[3], tiger ebony, and yucca and Pandanus species grew on its rocky sides and white-breasted sea eagles sailed off into the sky.

Basking in the Blue Lagoon, Manuel Pañares, 2015.

Approaching the ragged edge of the lagoon, I could see right through the crystalline water a profusion of vibrantly colored fishes, exotic corals and marine creatures like in a brilliant aquarium display. I slipped into the water and it felt wonderfully cold. We snorkeled and marveled at close quarters at the abundance of marine species of all kinds and shapes, in every color of the rainbow.

I held still and watched a rainbow of perky damselfish, spine-cheeked anemone fish, panda butterflyfish and angelfish parading about in brightly flashing aggregations above the clusters of corals and picking tidbits from the branches here and there. A pair of prominent Moorish idols swims gracefully and hovers over a purple-tip, white sea anemone, posing as if they were the royalty of the underwater world. I swam alongside a dazzling blue-barred parrotfish until I was face- to- face with a large snubnose grouper staring at me out of a hole, with a look that seems to ask, "Hey, wanna play a game of hide and seek?"

On the sandy bottom are peculiar-shaped sea stars. It was the very first time I have seen a mottled orange pentagon-shaped pin-cushion star[4]. I held it curiously in my hand, this sea star the shape of a pentagon. It did not look like a starfish at all, but more like a pincushion.

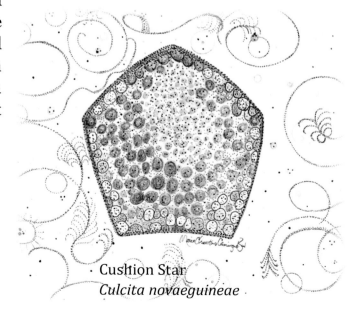

Cushion Star
Culcita novaeguineae

136

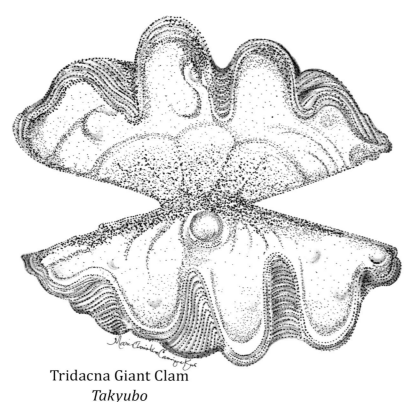

Tridacna Giant Clam
Takyubo

I came slowly near a colony of giant Tridacna clams[5] or *takyubo*, embedded into the corals, showing only their shining colored mantles.

They shut up when I tried to poke their gaping maws. To the left was a crowd of sea urchins or *tajum*, with exceptionally long, narrow, needle spines that vary from six to ten inches in length, gently waving amid stony corals in the shallow, sandy bottom. At a closer look, I was astonished to see an urchin releasing a smoky cloud of eggs, a miraculous burst of life!

But one of the rarest and most fascinating reef inhabitants I ever encountered while snorkeling deep in the heart of Bucas Grande, was the barrel-shaped, gelatinous chained salps, which may vary from a few millimeters to ten inches long. I reached out and touched these tunicates, champions of synchronized swimming, moving swiftly through sea currents like long strings of minuscule, inflatable, see-through floating beds.

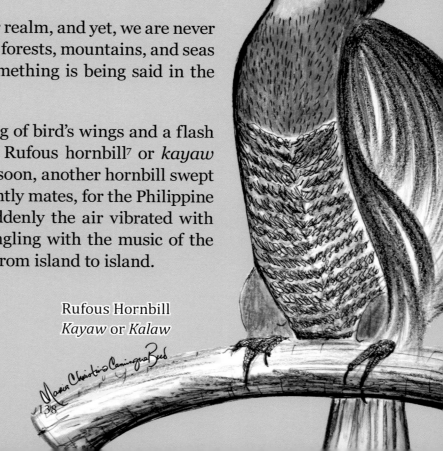

Here in Bucas Grande, nothing is as acutely audible as the sound of silence. Our boat guide would continually remind us to observe silence.

"There came, at times, from out of the silence, the eerie sound of a woman's voice singing out here in the wilderness," he told us. "The fisherfolk listened and were spellbound. In the past, Sohoton was devoid of human habitation but these fishermen told us they have heard a woman singing somewhere out there."

We are alone in this enchanted[6] water realm, and yet, we are never less alone than when we're alone. The forests, mountains, and seas have spirits of their own. *Listen*. Something is being said in the wind, the earth and the water.

The silence was broken by the beating of bird's wings and a flash of red darted among the trees as a Rufous hornbill[7] or *kayaw* alighted in the upper branches. Very soon, another hornbill swept through the canopy. They were evidently mates, for the Philippine hornbills usually travel in pairs. Suddenly the air vibrated with their booming calls, their voices mingling with the music of the winds, a rhapsodic rapture, echoing from island to island.

Rufous Hornbill
Kayaw or *Kalaw*

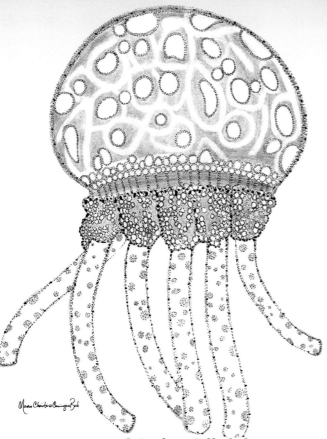

I shivered with excitement at the sights, scents and sounds before me. The all-white egrets and the dark-grey Eastern Pacific Reef-egret make a picturesque scene, bending their heads to feed on the mangroves[8]. A Brahminy kite or *banog* soars off into the bluest blue sky, and plummets to the water.

This is a timeless realm of rock, trees and water; as we paddled our kayaks across the blue lagoon we could see the pink, blue and golden, stingless jellyfish, some the size of plates, congregating by the hundreds, shimmering in the September sunlight. We spotted giant flying foxes[9], the world's largest fruit bats, wheeling in the sky and flipping over to roost upside down, its wings wrapped around its body, in the canopy of emergent trees.

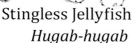

Stingless Jellyfish
Hugab-hugab

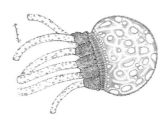

139

Bucas Grande echoes the dramatic natural beauty of El Nido in Palawan, in a smaller scale. Wind and waves sculpted these limestone islands and cliffs, as high as ten to 20 meters, cloaked in extensive surviving forests of *mangkono* or the rare Philippine Ironwood, *yakal, kamagong, lauaan, jamoyaon, maribojoc* pine and *kalingag* or cinnamon. Scarlet splashes of fire orchids contrasted against the dense greenery. One of the rare and endangered plants here is the Tropical Pitcher plant (*Nepenthes sp.*) that thrives up the rocky hill behind Hidden Island Resort in the Latasan and Bobon islets, which form part of Barangay Doña Helene, 15-20 minutes by boat from the port of Socorro, the southernmost and second largest town of Siargao Island in Surigao del Norte.

Tropical Pitcher Plant in Bucas Grande

Photo: Surigao del Norte Siargao Islands Protected Landscapes and Seascapes (SIPLAS Office, Dapa).

Socorro is also a place of historical interest on account of its association with the "Colorum uprising of 1924", where patriotic farm laborers and workers in Surigao rose in revolt against acts of oppression under American rule.[10]

One day, Roselyn Merlin of the Surigao City Tourism invited me to join her and School Directress Eunor Cortes of the Philippine Women's University (Surigao Campus) and heads of government agencies, tourism operators, and the media on a boat trip into Sohoton, where we stopped at the mouth of a shallow cave, set off on foot up a steep but short climb until we came out of an opening. I stared at it in wonder. There before me, for the first time, was a green lagoon, quiet and tranquil, shrouded in glistening tropical foliage. It was a place of enchantment, a Temple of Nature, an escape to a sublime realm.

One by one, my companions stood on the platform, some 15 ft. above water level, and somersaulted effortlessly into the water. I tarried a little while longer. It had been ten years since I last jumped from the Magpupungko Rock Formation and Natural Lagoon in Pilar, with my friends, Myra, Charina, and Siargao's junior surfing champs, Dodong, Elmer and Yokyok.

"We shall have to leave you now if you still can't make up your mind!" shouted somebody from the boat below.

In a moment, I gathered my guts and finally let go. *Wohoo!*

We swam in the glass-clear waters and explored water caverns that have lain here untouched since time immemorial. We swam excitedly towards Hagokan cave through a tiny opening above the water. I held my breath and went under. When I came up to the surface, it was totally dark and silent. I felt my way around the interior recesses and touched what seemed to be armors of mussels or *tayaba*, hundreds of them filling into every cranny and crevice! And just look at this luminous water! When the sunlight is refracted through the lagoon, the water glows with iridescent blue, and there seems a kind of magic portal drawn about the grotto, enclosing us in radiant blue light, like a dream

One never-to-be-forgotten summer, my long-time trusted boatman, *Tio* Arturo, my cousin, Mateo or Tiyoy, my high school friend, Faye, and I traveled to the remote island of Anajawan. We met the village chief, *Barangay* Captain Wilde Forcadilla and his wife, Florita, their children, and grandchildren, who offered to show us around the place and invited us for lunch. Such hospitality, I would say, is instinctive with the islanders. Although poverty is a fact of life over much of Anajawan and other rural villages, the astounding natural beauty of the islands of Siargao softens the shock of it and the world-famous, genuine Filipino friendliness, kindness and generosity reign supreme in the heart and home of everyone on the island.

We walked the interior of Anajawan where we discovered the Philippine National Leaf - *Anahaw* or fan palm, pandanus species and wild and precious shells – the large Helmet shell (Cassidae), locally called *lunga* or *budyong,* Tiger cowries and Triton Trumpet or *tambuli.*

Beneath the *talisay* trees, we ate lunch together on a large wooden table by the beach, the sea breeze in our faces. The *Kapitan's* family served us fresh seafood - squid, octopus, and *bangsi* or bluefish caught out by the reef. Later, we asked *Kapitan* Wilde to take us to the Sohoton Marine Reserve, south of the Siargao group of islands. Sohoton was just a short boat trip west of Anajawan Island. He agreed and we hopped on his small, twin-engine outrigger boat and crossed the open waters for an hour-and-a-half journey to Sohoton in Bucas Grande.

It was low tide when we reached Sohoton. We were lucky the tide was out so our passage was safe. Travelers to Sohoton must always deal with the question of weather, tides[11] and seasons of travel for as in any exertion, timing is everything.

There was no park ranger station then so we entered Sohoton freely. We fell silent, sensing the sacredness of the place as we drifted amidst cliffs, tidal caves and lush islands. We thought we were the only visitors to Sohoton until we came across two teen-age boys, Junrie and Dodie, leaping into the water, jumping and balancing acts upon the trees and rocks like gymnasts.

"Why don't you come and guide us?" I asked them.

It did not take long to persuade the young daredevils to join us. They gladly jumped into our boat and guided us inside the watery wilderness. Shortly, we entered a blue lagoon and *Kapitan* Wilde, our boatman, dropped anchor beside a half-submerged rock. We were in high spirits and savored our refreshingly cool swim and the extraordinarily beautiful setting.

Slowly and carefully, I swam out, farther and faster, away from my companions. I found myself swimming along with the current, floating on my back, enjoying the solace of nature. It was such a blissful sensation being carried along by the tide. On and on I went in that great flow, gliding swiftly backward through the water. Before long, the tide was rising quickly and in the next moment, I found myself being swept away by the tide, getting further away from the boat. I fought my way against the current and swam with all my might but the force of the rushing water was just too strong. I know I could not go back to the boat.

"Tiyoy, come and get me!" I cried out loud.

An expert swimmer, Tiyoy sprang into the water and swam straight towards me. I was treading water some 20 meters away from the boat. It was hard work but he was able to rescue me. We held on to each other until we reached the boat.

144

We made our way out of Sohoton in no time. We were just about to leave Bucas Grande, when it started to pour. The rain was coming down fast now. Our tiny craft waded into the swell and salt spray washed over the boat every few minutes, drenching *Kapitan* Wilde, Tiyoy, Faye and I. We were entirely at the mercy of the rain, wind, and waves, unable to do anything more than hang on and pray hard. We had no choice but to brave the stinging rain and the pitiless waves on a small pump boat with only a tarpaulin over our heads for cover and protection.

"Never again," Faye muttered, her face set in determination.

Finally, we reached the shores of my parents' hometown late in the afternoon. Wet to the skin and stiff and sore from head to foot, I drew a deep breath of relief and said a prayer of thanks for our safe landing after a tempestuous journey, battered by wind and rain. How I yearned for a long, hot bath and deep sleep. We disembarked at the wharf and walked slowly through the beach, still shivering with numbing cold.

Kanlanuk Falls tumble down the rocky hillside into several cascading streams and crystal pools. Pamosaingan, Bucas Grande, Siargao Islands Protected Landscapes and Seascapes (SIPLAS).

Photo: Cals Dantes

Diving into a garden of table corals in the Kanlanuk Sanctuary.
Kanlanuk Bay, Pamosaingan.
Bucas Grande, Siargao Islands Protected Landscapes and Seascapes (SIPLAS).

Photo: Cals Dantes

Christina Camingue Buo

F.L.Y. First Love Yourself, Manuel Pañares, 2016.

The Gift of Birds

Following the unbeaten path, we set out for an early morning walk into the lowland forest of Lobo, in the interior of Dapa[1], the principal town of Siargao. A semicircle of forested hills enclosed us in a hidden world which shelters a number of endemic and endangered species, including the Philippine tarsier and hornbill. Forming a great forest canopy is the *lauaan* (Philippine mahogany) and *yakal*, among the tallest of rainforest trees, rising to 24 - 30 meters, where the Brahminy kite or *banog* nests with its young.

We followed a dirt footpath and through tall coconuts, large droop *balete* or *diakit* trees, cogon grass, *achuete*, which is used as food coloring and dye, lavender-hued *hantutungan* flowers and *baliu* or pandanus palms, whose long, sharp, prickly leaves are woven into *banig* or traditional mats by the villagers. We walked for a kilometer to the starting point before we finally entered the forest.

I was shown around by forest ranger Lando Pobe who expertly points out the different plants, trees, and birds around us.

"We come here for regular inspection and at times, we spend the whole morning just listening to the birds," says Lando, whose ranger-guide expertise spans 15 years, including his stint with the Integrated Protected Areas System (IPAS) in the 1990s.

Further into the forest, we ventured, clambering over and under different trees - *duyok-duyok, yakal, lauaan, jamoyaon, himbabayod, diakit, sajapo, hagdang-uwak, ulingan/pag-oringon, sudiang, and pangi* trees, bathed here and there, in rays of filtered sunlight. Everywhere I see epiphytes or air plants on the branches and trunks of trees and other plants. Fan-like palmettos grow in the shade of molave, mahogany, *sejutis*. I found bird's nest ferns and fire orchids, blooming red and wild on the trail. Green and reddish-brown mosses, *agsam* ferns and *sagay* carpet the forest floor. I nearly overlooked a crushed, empty honeycomb at my feet, which is a source of food for some local folks.

I love watching the tiny leaf beetle enameled in a brilliant green color, and the big, blue butterfly, as they flit and fly past me. At a closer look, we spotted the exoskeleton or tough skin of an *organo*, or beetle on a leaf surface.

As we hike up and down through the forest, it is obvious that illegal logging still continues here on a small scale. And yet, the forest is still dense and one can easily get lost in this tangle of vegetation.

"If you get lost in these woods, you might end up in Tuboran in the neighboring town of Del Carmen or Maasin in Pilar," Lando told me. One trail links up with Del Carmen on the north and another to Pilar on the east part of Siargao Island.

For the next two kilometers, the rugged, narrow trail climbs to about 150 meters above sea level, and after hiking for an hour, we reach the Biodiversity Monitoring System or BMS Site, in the deepest part of the woods, seen by so few and rarely observed during daylight hours. It was cool and quiet. Not a breath of air is stirring and I can smell the humus and hear the buzzing of *gangis* and *amimispis* insects.

Suddenly, the forest comes alive with lyrical birdsong. My companions and I listen with delight as we picked out the songs of sunbirds or *siwit*, pied fantails or *palantigon*, Asian koel (cuckoo) or *bahaw,* the staccato of a *tiko* or flowerpecker, the liquid notes of a Philippine Glossy Starling or *lansijang,* the subtle *tilic tilic* of an unseen Tarictic hornbill and the mid-distant hooting of an owl.

Crrr crrr. I hear the cooing of wild doves or *alimokon.* The *tagkularaw, sayaw* and *git-git* chatter incessantly. That's a *tarungan.* It can make up several different sounds. "*Ka-law, ka-law,*" went the cackling calls of the Rufous hornbills, known to pair for life and a symbol of loyalty and dedication to the family.

PHOTO: Lando Pobe

Then along came a familiar, cheery, emphatic whistle. Is that a man whistling?

"No, it's the sound of *perot*, a common tailor bird," says Lando. We sat on a fallen *duyok-duyok* wood, under the *anislag* tree, and listened long and deep to the melodious and rapturous singing of birds in the wild.

Philippine Hanging Parrot
Kulasisi
Caridad, Pilar, Siargao Island
Photo: Christina C. Buo

I have loved birds all my life. It is my good luck to have spent most of my summers in my grandparents' home in Siargao, nature's wild wonderland fronting the Philippine Deep or Mindanao Trench in the Pacific Ocean. Among my earliest memories of birds are those of a flock of snowy-white reef egrets gliding high above us, while we swam in the sun-swept lagoon. We looked up to a cast of kites or *banog* circling the skies and in an instant one raptor plummets to the water to snag a fish! I remember those flitting cattle egrets that perch on the backs of the *carabao* or water buffalo, out in the farm and fields. I fondly recall those summer afternoons climbing up the hill, *Boyod ni Pongkoy*, to watch out for brilliant-hued kingfishers, brightly-colored sunbirds and other beautiful, strange and fascinating birds.

The wood swallow or *git-git* is one tiny, territorial bird with a larger-than-life character. One August afternoon, the local folks were treated to an impressive spectacle in the woods of Catabaan. A territorial battle between an avian David and Goliath was underway. A tiny, sturdy-beaked swallow attacked an intruding Large-billed crow or *uwak* and defended its territory and the airspace above it, with all its might. The gutsy swallow battled the sinister black crow, more than double its size, in a sensational, head-bumping chase until the big, black crow capitulated and *caw cawed* away

Just up the hill of San Ramon, Dapa, is a lovely path for a hiking and bird-watching. One afternoon, just as the sun was about to set, my active 68-year-old mom, my nurse-sister, Maie, and her colleagues at the Siargao District Hospital, Nurse couple Celia and Victor, and Medical Technologist Aida and I made our way to the top of the hill along a steep trail overgrown with scented *ilang-ilang* and shady, old trees. Near the ridge, the view looks out into a sweeping panorama of the town of Dapa, its church, The Santo Niño Parish, and belfry, the red roof of the old, Spanish-style municipal building or *tribunal*[2], its harbor and outlying islands glowing in the sunset. Adding a mysterious charm to the summery dusk, the *bahaw* or Asian koels (cuckoo) punctuated the air with their sweet, ascending notes. All up and down the hill, they sang in the sunset.

"You'd think the *bahaw* is a queer bird because it lays its eggs in another bird's nest," said Nurse Victor Comahig, who loves taking long hikes after work with his wife and fellow nurse, Celia. "The female *bahaw* approaches a suitable nest when the mother bird is away and leaves her brood there for the host bird to raise them."

Birds are like people. Some are brave, faithful and full of gallantry. Others are greedy and some birds, like the Asian koel or cuckoo, are cheeky opportunists.

Photo: Christina Buo

The hiking trail in San Ramon, Dapa is flanked by exotic, fragrant ilang-ilang, palms and shady old trees.

The nurses at the hospital have many stories to tell about birds dying of shock, or a sudden death, upon arrival. The hospital's doors and windows are made of glass, which creates the illusion of open space. "Apparently, the birds are taken by the illusion and keep hitting the glass only to be knocked down unconscious," my nurse-sister told me.

I was contemplating the beach in Travellers Beach Resort in the neighboring town of General Luna, when a Pacific Reef-egret or heron (dark morph) swept down on the shore, snatching up tidal flat-worms in the shallows. I try to be as unobtrusive as possible for she takes off in flight as soon as she senses a slight movement nearby.

One time, Dapa Vice-mayor Jun-jun Gonzales took my friends, Rosababy Recto, May Falcon, and I to Abukay Beach Resort, where we watched a flock of gray egrets on the Pisangan Reef at low tide. All of a sudden, a large Brahminy kite flew by, carrying a rodent in its claws.

"Want to take a walk?" my friend, Emarialyn Toloy-Kim, asked me one afternoon after we had our fill of fresh and sweet *butong* or coconut water and meat at her falcata plantation in Santa Rosa, Malinao, General Luna. As we were walking quietly through the ground, thickly sown with underbrush, I felt something move under my feet. I blindly stepped on a bird! It is almost invisible against the ground for the bird camouflaged the dense undergrowth. A night-flying Philippine nightjar, locally named *duktor*, rose abruptly before me, spread its long, patterned wings and flew away to the other side. After a light, floating glide, it came back to its ground roost. What an uplifting sight it is, circling and wheeling low and quietly on wings that span some six feet!

In Tawin-tawin, I met Junior, a young farmer who had found an owl or *kumotkot*. He was passing through a dense cogon field one late afternoon when he came upon a large hollow on the ground, the size of a barrel. Peering into it, he found himself crawling on his knees face to face with this thing with big eyes, staring back at him, flapping its wings noisily.

"I was scared. I thought it was an *ayok*[3]," says Junior, referring to an *aswang* or vampire-like creature in Filipino folklore. There sitting on a stinking nest heaped with *alimango* (crabs) and *ayasan* (shellfish) was a Philippine grass owl. It stood more than a foot-tall, the size of a *banog*, long-legged, white-spotted with a heart-shaped face, and a wingspan of more than three feet. It was a young owl, having not yet learned to fly. Finally, Junior swung at the bird even as its claws scraped him!

Female Asian Koel or cuckoo
Bahaw

Brahminy kite
Banog

On a fine summer afternoon, Junior joined me on a very long walk to the forest and marshlands of Sukbahaw in Malinao, to show me the communal roost of golden-crowned fruit bats hanging from trees. On our way back home, we heard the melancholic hooting of an unseen owl far away over a grove, in the gathering darkness. The sound still echoes in my mind to this day.

There is always something special about watching and listening to birds. It is like magic, music, and poetry in motion. Like trees or starlight, birds are healing balm to the soul. To see a shy Green-winged ground pigeon (*manatad*) swooping down on the secluded garden or a pair of rare coletos and hanging parrots feeding on the sweet fruits of the *manzanitas* tree just outside my window is to experience beauty, grace, and freedom enough to make the spirit fly.

Climb a nearly vertical, jungle-swathed hill in San Benito to get to Poneas Lake, a 3-hectare, brackish water lake teeming with crabs, *bangus, sigwel,* and *man-og.* Full of light reflecting the blue heavens and cone-shaped hills, Poneas Lake is a vision of sylvan serenity.

Poneas Lake, San Benito
Siargao Island

Photo: Cio Datan

Dwell in
Wonder

Parrotfish. Photo by Surigao City Tourism.

Nature speaks to us in its varied moods – rain or shine, storm, and calm. It speaks to us in the surging winds and waves, in the emerging and receding tides. Nature whispers something in a blooming pink rose and the chanting trees. Nature beams in the white, sweet-scented camia and *sampaguita* blooms, piping birds, and buzzing honeybees. It sings in the melody of water falling in translucent ribbons down a cliff and laughs merrily in a bubbly spring. It weaves magic in a patch of forest decked out with glowing fireflies, like a shower of stars, on a soft, cool summer evening. Nature speaks softly to us in a breath of a solemn night and in the rosy –purple light of dawn. Nature speaks to us all the time. Will we not stop, look and listen?

Behold the wonders of nature! See the world with new eyes and listen deeply to the voices of the sky, the earth, and the sea, for they have their own wisdom. Feel the joy in every birdsong. Feel the wonder of double rainbows above the sky. Feel the magic of a fluttering butterfly. Take a walk in the woods, roam the seas, soar into the skies, and feel the spell of the wild. Find the saving grace of nature and discover the living God of All Creation.

Nature is a teacher, a refuge, and sanctuary, a healing catalyst, a fount of wisdom and joy, a source of strength and a sacred conduit to God. Whenever I slip away into the woods for a walk among the birds and the trees, I feel a strong connection to everything and I can sense the power of the living God in all things. The Great Creator Spirit is palpably present in every flower, fruit, and blade of grass. My heart does a somersault every time I hear the Asian koels, coletos, and sunbirds singing a symphony of joy, like Beethoven's Spring Sonata. I look up with awe at the large and beautiful Narra, the Philippine National Tree, whose branches spread out like loving arms embracing me; a dear old friend from whom I could draw strength and solace. The longer I look and deeper I go I find the imprint of God's nature in creation.

Nature is you, me and us. We are all part of nature and creation. We have connections to all creatures, big and small. Everything is connected to everything else. Even the moon and the stars are related to us. The water from the earth takes us back to our beginnings and our natural roots as if we were returning home, to the primordial womb of life. Our spirits rise as we climb to the top of a rock or mountain. Something leaps inside of me as I behold the solitary eagle circling the skies or whenever I hear the resonant calls of the Philippine hornbills echoing between mountains. Like all living things, we expand under an infinite sky. We are warmed by the sun. We are ripened by the falling rain. We grow wild in the heart of a rainforest. We shine like the sun, moon, and stars. Like the colorful buds of summer, we burst to blossom, into radiant possibilities.

There is nothing like nature for inspiring a childlike sense of wonder and pure joy in every heart. Nature opens an ever new world to us if only we are awake to our senses. To those who lovingly seek her and commune with her eternal beauties, nature reveals her secrets, all her genius, and glory. The more we know about our natural world, the more we understand the vast interdependence of all living things and learn to appreciate, care and protect our precious and priceless natural heritage. When we cultivate a grateful love of life, we learn to live in harmony with nature and our lives become so much richer and fuller beyond measure.

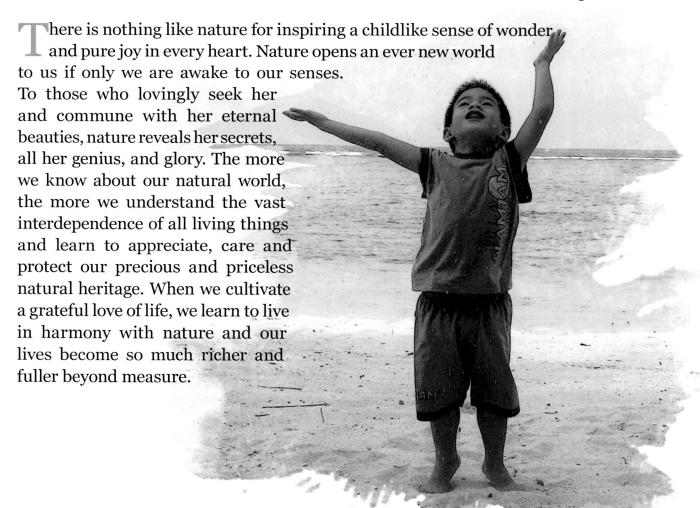

Luis Enrico playing with sand in Baybay, Burgos.
Photo: Christina C. Buo

Long-curling surf from the Pacific Ocean roll like liquid thunder and explodes into foam as it breaks onto the reef in Cloud 9, Catangnan in General Luna, Siargao.

Photo: Tonee Despojo

Notes and References

The White Lady and the *Tambis* Tree

1. *Tambis.* Scientific name: Syzygium aqueum.Δ It's also called wax jambu, water rose apple or water apple in English.

2. *Plaza* or town park. The wide open space bounded by roads and adjacent to the civic and ecclesiastical buildings of a town or city and intended for political or social activities. In the Ordenanza of 1573 or the Laws of the Indies, the plaza was the starting point in the creation of a town or city.#

3. *Amor-seco.* Spanish for love grass. A type of grass found throughout the Philippines in open places at low and medium elevations, with seeds that stick to one's clothing.

4. *Lola* is the Filipino term for grandmother. *Lolo* means grandfather.

5. *Pantaw* (Surigaonon dialect). Dirty kitchen or the back porch, with a traditional water pump, where household chores are done.

Δ Department of Environment and Natural Resources (DENR) Adm. Order No. 63 (2000). Provincial Environment and Natural Resources Office (PENRO)- Surigao del Norte, Siargao Islands Protected Landscapes and Seascapes (SIPLAS).

Fernandez, Rino D.A. (2015). *Diksiyonaryong Biswal Ng Arkitekturang Filipino - A Visual Dictionary on Filipino Architecture.* Manila: University of Santo Tomas.

6. *Tagnijogan na kayabang* (Surigaonon cuisine). Boiled beach crab steeped in thick coconut milk sauce.^

7. *Tinuya na bayo with tangyad* (Surigaonon cuisine). Needlefish soup with lemon grass and various spices.^

8. *Pinaksiw na buntog* and *heringero* (Surigaonon cuisine). Local fishes stewed in vinegar and garlic. *Buntog* belongs to the parrotfish family and *heringero* is Emperor Bream.^

9. *Carnaba* is the local term for *Cardaba (Cardava)* banana, a type of plantain that Filipinos use for cooking. *Saba* is another (commercial) type of banana plantain.

10. *Frigidaire* is a popular American brand of refrigerator and the first commercially available refrigerator in the Philippines.

11. *Tia* and *Tio* are the Surigaonon terms for Aunt and Uncle. It is a respectful form of address to a mature, elderly woman or man who is a relative or a friend of the family.

12. *Jamoyaon* is the Surigaonon name for the Molave tree. Scientific name: Vitex parviflora. Molave or *tugas* belongs to the Premium Philippine tree species.Δ *Jamoyaon* is the name of a *barangay* in the municipality of Del Carmen, Siargao, named after Our Lady of Mount Carmel, the Patroness of the Carmelite Monks. It was formerly known as Numancia. The area abounds in *Jamoyaon*, which is noted among the seafaring and fishing folks in Siargao for its use as hull planks of the native boats or *banca* because of its durability and resistance to seawater corrosion.√

13. *Sala* (Spanish). Living room or reception room.

---

^ Siargao and Bucas Grande Islands Sub-Provincial Fisheries, Dapa, Surigao Del Norte.

√ Fernando A. Almeda, Jr., Founding President of The Surigaonon Heritage Studies and Research Center, Surigao City, Philippines, Personal interview, 23 August 2017.

14. *Ayok* is the local name for a witch in Siargao, otherwise called *aswang* in Filipino.

15. *Sigbin* is the pet creature of a witch.

16. *Duwende* or Philippine dwarf. These tiny creatures live in homes under the ground and pass by magic through the holes in termite mounds.Ø

17. *Santelmo* or St. Elmo's Fire. In Siargao, many folks have claimed to have seen these flaming masses or orbs of light which are believed to be ghostly apparitions. Science, on the other hand, attributes it to an electrical phenomenon.

18. *Kapre* is a cigar-smoking, hairy giant or black spirit who dwells in a *balete* or banyan or a big tree. He appears under a new moon and a soft shower. Arabs call him *kafir* and Spaniards *cafre*.Ø

19. *Nipa hut.* Indigenous house of the Philippines with a thatched roof and walls made out of *nipa*, coconut lumber or bamboo.

Ø Ramos, Maximo D. (1990). *The Creatures of Midnight*. Manila: Phoenix Publishing House, Inc., and Maximo D. Ramos.

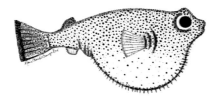

My First Pufferfish

1. *Purok* 2 (Dos) is one of five smaller administrative divisions of the town center or *poblacion* of General Luna in Siargao Island.

2. *Siesta.* Post-lunch nap.

3. *Barangay* is a basic socio-political unit in the Philippines which is ruled by a chieftain or *Kapitan. Barangay* comes from the word *balanghai* or *balangay* (boathouse), an impressive boat approximately 25 meters in length and carbon-dated to 320 AD, that was built entirely of wood and used for seafaring by the ancient Kingdom of Butuan.* Throughout Sotheast Asia and the world, it is only in the Philippines where a flotilla of such prehistoric wooden boats are known to exist. The National Museum of the Philippines excavated and conserved three *Balanghai* boats in Butuan and in 1986, Philippine President Corazon C. Aquino declared these boats as National Cultural Treasures by virtue of Presidential Proclamation No. 86.^

4. *Atis.* Sugar-apple fruit.

5. *Caimito.* Star-apple fruit.

6. *Carabao,* locally called *kabaw,* is the National Animal of the Philippines. It is called water buffalo in English.

7. *Sarok* or *Salakot* (Tagalog). Mushroom-shaped, native Filipino hat of woven bamboo strips.

8. *Buyo* or *sundang. Bolo* or long knife also used as farming implement.

9. *Nipa (Nypa fruiticans)* is a tropical palm with a short trunk and broad, pinnate leaves that grow abundantly along rivers and estuaries, its leaves are utilized both as roofing and walling materials.*

10. *Buwa.* Baby hammock made from used cotton blankets or *sako sa harina* (flour sack cloth).

11. *Baliu* is a member the Pandan family which is used in making traditional, hand-woven *banig* or sleeping-mats in Siargao. In the village of Caridad in Pilar, a group of women weavers use *alahiwan* plant to make traditional *pitate* mats.

12. *Atabay* or deep well.

13. *Kalachuchi* or frangipani, also known as plumeria.

14. *Sala.* Spanish for the living room. The central room in a Filipino house often facing the street or plaza and is used as the family's leisure and social activities' room.*

15. *Abaca* (Musa textilis)^ or Manila hemp, is a native fiber from a banana species. From the abaca or hemp fibers, rope is manufactured.

16. *Kinhason* and *tagitis* are edible marine shells.

17. *Ibis, dumod-ot, ito, agak. Ibis* means baby *hipon or shrimp. Dumod-ot* (silver-lined herring), *ito* and *agak* (siganid fingerlings) are small–sized marine fishes commonly found near the surface of the water in Malinao, General Luna. Like *poot-poot, dumod-ot* and *agak* are used in making traditional fish paste or *ginamos* in Siargao Island.#

18. *Lusay* or seagrass. Scientific name: Thalassia hemprichii. This common seagrass has leaf blades that are linear and distinctly scythe-shaped.Δ

19. Pufferfish is called *butete* in the local dialect. Family Tetraodontidae. These fishes can inflate their bodies with air and water to an almost circular shape as a defense mechanism. The viscera of most puffers contain an alkaloid poison, tetrodotoxin. In Japan, puffer flesh is considered a delicacy when prepared correctly without the viscera.Δ

---

* Fernandez, Rino D.A. (2015). *Diksiyonaryong Biswal Ng Arkitekturang Filipino - A Visual Dictionary on Filipino Architecture.* Manila: University of Santo Tomas.
^ Cembrano, Margarita R. (1998). *Patterns of the Past: The Ethno Archaeology of Butuan.* Manila: The National Museum of the Philippines.
# Siargao and Bucas Grande Islands Sub-Provincial Fisheries, Dapa, Surigao Del Norte.
Δ White, Alan T. (2001). *Philippine Coral Reefs: A Natural History Guide, (New and Revised Edition).* Manila: Bookmark, Inc. and Sulu Fund for Marine Conservation Foundation.

Seraphim, the Turtle- Dove

1. *Tukmo* is the local name for turtle-dove in Siargao Island.

2. *Plaza* or town park. An open public square that is adjacent to both major roads and prestigious civic and religious buildings.#

3. *Poblacion* refers to the central area of the municipal town of General Luna which is made up of five smaller districts: *Purok Uno* (1), *Purok Dos* (2), *Purok Tres* (3), *Purok Cuatro* (4) and *Purok Cinco* (5).

4. *Tabanog* is the local term for kite.

5. *Gumamela* or hibiscus flower.

6. *Dap-dap*. Scientific name: Erythrina orientalis. Lesser-used Philippine tree species. ∞

7. *Purok Tres* (3) is one of five smaller divisions of the *poblacion* or town center of General Luna in Siargao Island.

Fernandez, Rino D.A. (2015). *Diksiyonaryong Biswal Ng Arkitekturang Filipino - A Visual Dictionary on Filipino Architecture*. Manila: University of Santo Tomas.

∞ DENR Adm. Order No. 63 (2000). PENRO - Surigao del Norte, Siargao Islands Protected Landscape and Seascape (SIPLAS).

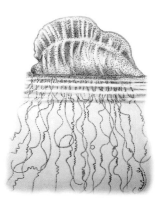

Portuguese Man-of-War

1. *Pisangan Reef.* Coral reef serving as a barrier protecting the wide cove of the town of General Luna from the giant swells of the Pacific Ocean.*

2. *Copra.* Dried coconut kernels from which oil and other useful substances are obtained.

3. *Lajag.* Native sailboat.

4. *Siakoy* is the local name for twisted sugar doughnuts, an all-time Filipino favorite *merienda* or snack.

5. *Binignit.* Traditional coconut milk-based dessert with banana, sweet potato, *ube* or purple yam, jackfruit and pearl *sago*.

6. *Apo.* Filipino for grandchildren.

7. *Sungka.* A game on a wooden board with 16 depressions cut into it. During the 1980s in the town of General Luna, Siargao, *sungka* was played using small gold ringers and other Indo-Pacific cowries or *sigay*. This traditional Filipino board game is similar to *congkak* or *congklak*, a mancala game of Malay origin which is played in Malaysia, Singapore, Southern Thailand, Brunei and Indonesia.^

8. *Kasing* is the local name for a wooden spinning top.

9. *Bato-lata.* Visayan term of *tumbang preso* in Tagalog, an outdoor children's game using a slipper or *tsinelas* to knock down an empty tin can.

10. *Dakop-dakop.* Popular outdoor children's game in the Philippines which is similar to the game "Tag, you're it!".

11. *Tago-tago.* Hide and seek or *taguan*.

12. *Tubig-tubig* is the local version of *patintero*, an outdoor children's game in the Philippines.

13. *Flores de Mayo* or or Flowers of May is a traditional and popular Catholic devotion celebrated in honor of the Blessed Virgin Mary for the whole month of May.

14. *Cantora.* Spanish for female singer.

15. Visayan hymn to the Blessed Virgin Mary:

Adto Na kami Maria, Adios kanimo, Señora
Ug ayaw kami hikalimti, sa kadautan panlabani
Adto Na kami, Adios, Maria, Adios, Adios, kanimo, Señora

English Translation

Goodbye to you, Blessed Virgin Mary, Farewell to you, Our Lady
And don't forget us, from evil protect us,
Goodbye and Farewell, Blessed Virgin Mary, Farewell, Farewell to you, Our Lady.

16. Philippine calamansi or *lemonsito*. Native lime.

---

* General Luna, Siargao. "Municipality of General Luna Comprehensive Development Plan (2010-2016)."
^ Wikepedia Contributors. "Congkak." Wikepedia, The Free Encyclopedia. Wikipedia, The Free Encyclopedia, 09 Sept. 2017. Web. 09 Sept. 2017. <https:// en.wikipedia.org/wiki/ Congkak>

Firefly Dances

1. *Poblacion* refers to the central area of the town of General Luna which is divided into five units: *Purok Uno (1)*, *Purok Dos (2)*, *Purok Tres (3)*, *Purok Cuatro (4)* and *Purok Cinco (5)*.

2. *Kalachuchi* is another name for frangipani or plumeria.

3. Parish Church is a church strategically built at the heart of the town and it is intended for a particular ecclesiastical unit, such as city or town, under the jurisdiction of the resident priest assigned by the bishop.*

4. *Bahay kubo,* cube-shaped house. A common type of dwelling in lowland and coastal areas during the pre-Hispanic Philippines. *Bahay* is a Tagalog word for a house while *kubo* is from Spanish *cubo*, meaning a cube. It is often built with whole bamboo or tree branches as a structural framework and finished with bamboo strips for floors, palm leaves for the roof, and bamboo strips or palm leaves for walls.*

5. *Lamparilla.* Small glass oil lamp.

6. *Katunggan.* Surigaonon for mangrove swamp, or *bakhawan.*

7. *Abaca* or Manila hemp. It is said that the best and strongest ropes are made from Philippine hemp.

---

* Fernandez, Rino D.A. (2015). *Diksiyonaryong Biswal Ng Arkitekturang Filipino - A Visual Dictionary on Filipino Architecture.* Manila: University of Santo Tomas.

Bat Girl

1. *Bahay kubo* is a common type of dwelling during the Pre-Hispanic Philippines. It is a one-room house raised above the ground to protect the dwellers from the dampness and humidity of the earth.^

2. Philippine Tarsier. Scientific name: Tarsius syrichta. It is among the Philippines' Terrestrial Threatened Species as defined in Republic Act No.9147, otherwise known as the Wildlife Resources Conservation and Protection Act.# It was considered among the world's 25 Most Endangered Primates (2014-2016 but removed from the 2016–2018 list) by the International Union for Conservation of Nature (IUCN). Tarsiers are found in Bohol, Samar, Leyte, Basilan, Dinagat Island, Lake Sebu in South Cotabato and Maitum in Sarangani.* Tarsiers also live in the forests of Mt. Mayapay in Butuan City, Agusan del Norte and tribal farmers are appealing to the public and private sectors to help them save the tarsier's forest habitat which is threatened with slash-and-burn farming, firewood gathering and timber poaching!

3. Giant flying fox. Scientific name: Pteropus vampyrus. Listed among the country's Terrestrial Threatened Species as defined in Republic Act No. 9147, also known as the Wildlife Resources Conservation and Protection Act.#

---

^Fernandez, Rino D.A. (2015). *Diksiyonaryong Biswal Ng Arkitekturang Filipino – A Visual Dictionary on Filipino Architecture.* Manila: University of Santo Tomas.

\# DENR Adm. Order No.15 (2004). PENRO - Surigao del Norte SIPLAS (Dapa, Siargao).

* Tacio, Henrylito.(2010). S*aving Tarsier from Extinction due to Deforestation, Illegal Logging.* Retrieved from https://www.gaiadiscovery.com/nature-biodiversity/saving-tarsier-from-extinction-due-to-deforestation-illegal.html

! Caraga Aksyon Balita (bilingual weekly newspaper), Surigao City: June 5-11, 2017.

Echoes of Tawin-Tawin Creek

1. *Pijapi* or *piapi, pagatpat* and *bakhaw* are three common mangroves in the Philippines. *Pijapi (bungalon).* Scientific name: Avicennia marina. *Pagatpat.* Scientific name: Sonneratia alba. *Bakhaw.* Scientific name: Rhizophora species. ∝

2. *Nipa.* "Nypa fruticans" is a tropical palm with a short trunk and broad pinnate leaves that grow abundantly along rivers and estuaries, its leaves are utilized both as roofing and walling materials.∇

3. Some of the most powerful typhoons in the Philippines enter through the northeastern approach of Surigao. It was through this corridor of the Pacific that Ferdinand Magellan first sailed into the Philippines in 1521 after a long, and perilous voyage. #

4. *Duwende* are small creatures, much like goblins or dwarfs, living underground. They may be kind or mischievous, depending on how the person has treated them, and like to be left alone. Filipinos believe that uttering *"tabi tabi po"* before entering suspected duwende territories will not disturb them.~

∝Primavera, J.H. "Stop seafront planting of bakhaw propagules." *Philippine Daily Inquirer,* 28 Feb. 2015, http://business.inquirer.net/187523/stop-seafront-planting-of-bakhaw-propagules/

∇Fernandez, Rino D.A. (2015). *Diksiyonaryong Biswal Ng Arkitekturang Filipino – A Visual Dictionary on Filipino Architecture.* Manila: University of Santo Tomas.

#Almeda, Jr., Fernando A. (1993). *Story of a Province: Surigao Across the Years.* Manila: The Philippine National Historical Society and the Heritage Publishing House.

~ Clark, Jordan. (2017). *Creatures & Mythical Beings from Philippine Folklore & Mythology.* Retrieved from https://www.aswangproject.com/creatures-mythical-beings-philippine-folklore-mythology/

A Song in the Wind

1. *Sala* is short for the Spanish term *sala de estar* or living room. The central room in a Filipino house often facing the street or plaza and is used as the family's leisure and social activities' room. ^

2. *Bangkay* or *Bangkal, Kaatoan.* Scientific name: Nauclea orientalis. It belongs to the Furniture/ construction hardwood Philippine tree species.*

3. Gmelina arborea or Yemane. The roots, bark, sap and leaves of the Gmelina Tree have medicinal uses.

4. Mahogany. Scientific name: Swietenia mahagoni. It belongs to the Furniture/ construction hardwood Philippine tree species.*

5. *Narra* is the National Tree of the Philippines. Scientific name: Pterocarpus indicus. It belongs to the Premium Philippine tree species.* Classified under category A – Critically Endangered Species in the DENR's National List of Threatened Philippine Plants and their Categories.

6. *Baroto.* A non-motorized *banca* or boat, which may or may not be equipped with outrigger or *katig*, and is propelled by a wooden steering oar or *bugsay*.

---

^ Fernandez, Rino D.A. (2015). *Diksiyonaryong Biswal Ng Arkitekturang Filipino – A Visual Dictionary on Filipino Architecture.* Manila: University of Santo Tomas.

* DENR Adm. Order No. 63 (2000). Provincial Environment and Natural Resources Office (PENRO)- Surigao del Norte, Siargao Islands Protected Landscape and Seascape (SIPLAS).

The Medicine Woman
A Tribute to the *Manhilot* or *Albularyo*

1. *Bakasyonista.* Vacationers or holidaymakers.

2. *Manhilot* or *Albularyo (Herbolario).* A traditional chiropractor or herbal healer expert in the use of medicinal plants and trees.

3. *Manang* (female) is a local honorific used when addressing a person (relative or not) older than the speaker. *Manoy* is the male counterpart.

4. *Bahay kubo.* A common type of dwelling in lowland and coastal areas during the Pre-Hispanic Philippines. The *bahay kubo* has three distinct horizontal divisions, namely: the stilts or posts *(haligi)*, the one-room upper living unit and the steep roof. The posts are often covered or enclosed with bamboo latticework to serve as usable space underneath the house for house implements or livestock.*

5. *Purok 3 (Tres).* One of five smaller divisions of the town center or poblacion of General Luna, Siargao Island.

---

* Fernandez, Rino D.A. (2015). *Diksiyonaryong Biswal Ng Arkitekturang Filipino – A Visual Dictionary on Filipino Architecture.* Manila: University of Santo Tomas.

Christmas in Anajawan

1. *Isda sa bato* or *lapu-lapu* is known as Grouper in English.

2. *Lunga* or *Budyong.* Helmet shell. Genus cassis. Protected under the Philippine Fisheries Code of 1998 or Republic Act 8550 (amended in 2015 as RA 10654, "An Act to Prevent, Deter and Eliminate Illegal, Unreported, and Unregulated Fishing). The species is also protected under the Convention on International Trade in Endangered Species of Wild Fauna and Flora (CITES). The Philippines is a signatory to the treaty. ^

3. *Tambuli.* Trumpet shell. Genus Triton or Charonia Tambuli. Protected Philippine Aquatic Wildlife.^

4. Siargao is part of Surigao del Norte Province which falls under Type II climate, with no pronounced dry season, but with maximum rain period from December to March in time with the Northeast Monsoon or *Amihan* months. Temperature ranges from 23.6°C to as high as 31.3 °C annually. January has the highest amount of rainfall and lowest in May. The high waves and strong current from the Pacific are extremely hazardous at certain times of the year, especially during typhoon season (November-December).*

---

^Siargao and Bucas Grande Islands Sub-Provincial Fisheries, Dapa, Surigao del Norte.
* Siargao and Bucas Grande Islands Master Plan 2008-2020, PENRO – Surigao del Norte Siargao Islands Protected Landscapes and Seascapes or SIPLAS.

5. *Tuba.* Palm toddy or fermented coconut wine.

6. *Aparador* is Spanish for china cabinet.

7. *Sarok* is a mushroom-shaped native hat of woven bamboo strips. *Salakot* in Tagalog.

8. *Dayag asaw* or sea snakes are venomous but the venom of some is not strongly toxic to humans while that of others is more powerful than the cobra's. The Laticauda colubrina (Banded sea snake) is normally seen on the shallow reef flat, among corals on the outer reef or crawling on shoreline rocks or cliffs. The Hyrdophis species comes periodically to the surface to breathe and lives on shallow or midwater reefs. Sea snakes are sought for their skin and meat. They have been exploited and are now rare in the Philippines. ~

9. Surigaonon is the dialect spoken in Surigao del Norte Province in Caraga, Philippines.

10. *Adobong Baboy.* Stewed pork in a mixture of soy sauce, garlic, and vinegar.

11. *Abuhan.* Cooking area. An elevated earthen fireplace with the stone stove for cooking and layers of open shelves for drying firewood and smoking fish.#

~ White, Alan T. (2001). *Philippine Coral Reefs: A Natural History Guide, (New and Revised Edition)*. Manila: Bookmark, Inc. and Sulu Fund for Marine Conservation Foundation.

#Fernandez, Rino D.A. (2015). *Diksiyonaryong Biswal Ng Arkitekturang Filipino – A Visual Dictionary on Filipino Architecture*. Manila: University of Santo Tomas.

12. *Biko na linunokan.* Surigaonon term for sticky rice cooked with coconut milk topped with grated, caramelized coconut.

13. *Manoy.* A local honorific used when addressing a male person (relative or not), older than the speaker. *Mano* refers to an older brother or male relative. *Mana* refers to an older sister or an older female relative.

14. *Santelmo.* A supernatural being in Philippine folklore and mythology. Stories of *Santelmo* (or *Santilmo*) say that it is the spirit of a person who has died near a river, lake, ocean, or during heavy rains. The lost soul appears as a ball of fire and some say it seeks revenge on those who may have done him wrong, while others claim the soul is seeking peace. ^

15. *Fiesta.* A religious and cultural feast held in barangays, towns or cities in the predominantly Catholic Philippines to honor its patron saint, celebrate a bountiful harvest or commemorate its history and culture with a High Mass *(Misa cantada),* processions, plays, rituals, trade exhibits, concerts, pageants, and contests.

---

^ Clark, Jordan. (2017). *Santelmo: Rekindling Philippine Mythology,* Retrieved from https://www.aswangproject.com/santelmo/

Who Hitch-hikes in the Highway?

1. *Dili ingon nato.* Preternatural beings or invisible entities of another dimension.

2. *Agta.* In Philippine Folk Literature: The Legends, compiled & edited by Prof. Damiana L. Eugenio, the Mother of Philippine Folklore, she classifies *Agta* as under "Miscellaneous Supernatural Beings" described as "black giants of great strength," who, old folks believe, sit on the road to dry themselves. When the drivers blow their horns, the *Agta* get out of the way & no accident happens, but when drivers do not blow their horns, the *Agta* simply elbow the vehicles aside & they crash.*

3. *Kapre.* The Creatures of Midnight Author Maximo D. Ramos classified *kapres* under "Philippine demons" described as a dark-skinned, rough and hairy man as tall as the tree beside which he stands. He smokes a big cigar and assumes the shapes of animals or people. The *Ibanag* Tribe of Northern Luzon calls him, *ammalabi,* "the ever-changing one."^

4. *Salo –salo.* Get-together over a meal.

5. *Lechon.* Spit-roasted suckling pig.

6. *Kinilaw.* Dish of edible raw fish or seafood marinated in vinegar or *suka* and *calamansi* (native lime) and mixed with spices. Traditionally, islanders eat *kinilaw* of fresh *gangis* or surgeon fish, tuna or *bulis, langog* and *danggit* (siganids).

---

* Eugenio, Damiana L. (2002). *Philippine Folk Literature: The Legends.* Manila: University of the Philippines Press.

^ Ramos, Maximo D. (1990). *The Creatures of Midnight.* Manila: Phoenix Publishing House, Inc., and Maximo D. Ramos.

A Walk in the Woods

1. *Tapahan.* Tiny wooden shed used for making or storing copra or coconut kernels. The Municipalities of Del Carmen, General Luna and Dapa are the major coconut-producing areas in the islands.#

2. *Diakit* or *Balete* Tree. A large tree with oblong-shaped leaves. It is said to be the domicile of the *kapre* and other dark creatures in Philippine folklore.

3. Philippine tarsiers are facing threats of slash-and-burn farming, firewood gathering and timber poaching in the forests of Mt. Mayapay, Butuan City, Agusan del Norte in the Caraga Region.Δ

4. Golden-crowned fruit bat. Scientific name: Acerodon jubatus. Listed as endangered in the National List of Terrestrial Threatened Species and their Categories as described in RA 9147, or the Wildlife Resources Conservation and Protection Act.^

5. Werebeast or *Aswang na lakaw.* In his study of Philippine demonological lore, Dr. Maximo Ramos refers to the "werebeast" as an ordinary person by day who grows monstrous on some nights, assumes the shape of a fierce dog, cat, goat or cattle, and attacks wayfarers at night.*

Siargao and Bucas Grande Islands Master Plan 2008-2020, PENRO– Surigao del Norte (SIPLAS).

Δ Caraga Aksyon Balita, Surigao City: June 5-11, 2017.

^ DENR Adm. Order No. 15 (2004) PENRO - Surigao del Norte SIPLAS (Dapa, Siargao).

* Ramos, Maximo D. (1991). *Remembrance of Lents Past & other Essays.* Manila: Phoenix Publishing House, Inc., & Maximo D. Ramos.

6. The *tianak* usually appears as a baby to attract the attention of passersby, but when one makes the mistake of taking it up and cuddling it, it bites the person and shows itself in its true hideous form.=

7. *Aswang*, locally called *Ayok*. Shapeshifting demon, humanlike by day but transforms into different monstrous forms at night. *Aswang* can change from a human to an animal form, usually as a bat, a pig or a black dog. *Aswang* is a generic name for Filipino vampiric creatures, such as *Manananggal*, etc.@

Journey into the Wild

1. Bucas Grande is a micro archipelago about 35 miles southeast of Surigao City, but barely six miles across a channel to the southern mainland of the province of Surigao del Norte. On both sides of Bucas, two of its oldest and biggest villages, Socorro and Pamosaingan, look out into the open sea. Spaniards call it "Bucas" because it's the opening of the great passage into the Pacific Ocean towards the southern route all the way to Cape San Agustin (Davao Oriental), the old gateway to the country. Siargao is separated from Bucas by a channel.^ Siargao and Bucas Grande Islands are located at Dinagat Sound, off the northeastern coast of Mindanao, part of the province of Surigao del Norte, one of the five provinces comprising Caraga Region. There are nine (9) municipalities divided into 131 barangays.*

= Eugenio, Damiana L. (2002). *Philippine Folk Literature: The Legends*. Manila: University of the Philippines Press.

@Clark, Jordan. (2017). *Creatures & Mythical Beings from Philippine Folklore & Mythology*. Retrieved from https://www.aswangproject.com/creatures-mythical-beings-philippine-folklore-mythology/

^Almeda, Jr., Fernando A. (2017). *The History of a Province: Surigao Across the Years (6th Edition)*. Manila: Vicarish Publication and Trading, Inc.

* Siargao and Bucas Grande Islands Master Plan 2008-2020, Provincial Environment & Natural Resources Office (PENRO) – Surigao del Norte SIPLAS (Dapa, Siargao Island).

2. The Philippines is divided into 15 Biogeographic Zones (BZ), which includes the Siargao Islands Protected Landscapes and Seascapes (SIPLAS), one of three priority protected areas in Mindanao BZ.* SIPLAS covers three (3) bio-diverse ecosystems: an extensive system of mangroves of almost pure stand of *Rhizophora apiculata* (the largest in Mindanao), pristine coral reef complex Δ and a terrestrial ecosystem. It is home to 123 species of flora and some 85 bird species, 21 mammal species, 54 species of seaweed/algae and 8 species of sea grasses.*

3. Philippine ironwood or *mangkono/magcono*. Scientific name: Xanthostemon verdugonianus.# Now endangered, the *mangkono* is the hardest known species of wood and is considered to be more enduring than steel.

4. The distinctive pillow or pin- cushion sea star, Culcita, has no apparent arms and looks like a flattened sphere with a green to red quilt-like pattern.~

Δ Knipp, Steven. (1998). *Our Natural Heritage: The Protected Areas of the Philippines.* Manila: Department of Environment and Natural Resources (DENR) and Philippine Airlines Foundation.

DENR Adm. Order No.63 (2000). PENRO- Surigao del Norte (SIPLAS) (Dapa, Siargao).

~ White, Alan T. (2001). *Philippine Coral Reefs: A Natural History Guide, (New and Revised Edition).* Manila: Bookmark, Inc. and Sulu Fund for Marine Conservation Foundation.

5. The largest of all bivalves, the True giant clam *takyubo/ taklobo* can reach over 200kg (animal & shell) but has become locally extinct in many areas and very rare in the Indo-Pacific.~ Giant clams are protected under Philippine Fisheries Admin. Order 208, Section 97 of RA8550 & listed in the Convention on the International Trade in Endangered Species of Wild Fauna and Flora (CITES), Appendix II.∂

6. Bucas Grande Island is truly a retreat for weary souls. Perhaps because of its serenity and silence, it is reputed to be an enchanted place.^^

7. *Kayaw (Kalaw)* or Rufous Hornbill. Also known as the Philippine hornbill. Listed as Vulnerable in the National List of Terrestrial Threatened Species.∇

8. The overall mangrove cover in Siargao and Bucas Grande Islands is approximately 9,000 has. The largest stretch is located in Del Carmen, covering almost 4,000 hectares.* The mangroves of Del Carmen and San Benito provide sanctuary to the endangered saltwater crocodile.

9. The Giant flying fox belongs to the "other Threatened species".∇ There is a large community of fruit-eating bats known as flying foxes in the Sohoton area.∆ Siargao is also home to the endangered Golden-crowned fruit bat.

~ White, Alan T. (2001). *Philippine Coral Reefs: A Natural History Guide.* Manila: Bookmark, Inc. and Sulu Fund for Marine Conservation Foundation.
∂ Siargao and Bucas Grande Islands Sub-Provincial Fisheries Office, Dapa, Surigao del Norte.
^^Almeda, Jr., Fernando A. (1993), *The Story of a Province: Surigao Across the Years.* Manila: Philippine National Historical Society and the Heritage Publishing House.
∇ DENR Adm. Order No. 15 (2004). PENRO- Surigao del Norte SIPLAS (Dapa, Siargao).

10. When it was yet a barrio of Dapa, Socorro was the hotbed of the historical "Colorum uprising".√ The struggle for freedom and liberty among the farmers and laborers in Surigao led to a bloody rebellion, the Colorum Uprising of 1924, against American colonial forces.

11. The ocean currents are strong around Siargao and Bucas Grande Islands brought about by the influence of the winds and currents of the Pacific Ocean. The high waves and strong current are extremely hazardous especially during typhoon season (Nov.-Dec.). The islands have maximum tide amplitude of 1.5 m and a minimum of 0.5 m.* During the monsoon season, devastating typhoons from the Pacific would visit the islands and leave in its wake so much destruction.^^ The Province of Surigao del Norte lies at the rim of the Philippine Deep, located about 35 miles east of Siargao Islands. It has a depth of 35,400 feet and has been observed as the epicenter of frequent earthquakes along the coast of Mindanao.^

√ Sering, Jose C.(1998).*Reminiscences: An Autobiography of Gov. Jose C. Sering.* Surigao City: Siargao Historical and Cultural Foundation.

* Siargao and Bucas Grande Islands Master Plan 2008-2020, Provincial Environment and Natural Resources Office (PENRO) - Surigao del Norte SIPLAS (Dapa, Siargao Island).

^^Almeda, Jr., Fernando A. (1993), *The Story of a Province: Surigao Across the Years.* Manila: Philippine National Historical Society and the Heritage Publishing House.

^ Almeda, Jr., Fernando A. (2017). *The History of a Province: Surigao Across the Years (6th Edition).* Manila: Vicarish Publication and Trading,Inc.

The Gift of Birds

1. The town of Dapa got its name during the moro raids when the inhabitants around the shores of the island took refuge in a cave and hid in the fields to escape raiders.^ In the local dialect, *dapa* means "to get down on one's hands and knees".

2. The old *municipio* in Dapa called the *tribunal* which was built during the Spanish times still stands and houses some government offices.^

3. *Ayok* is the local term for *aswang*. It is a generic name for Filipino vampiric creatures, such as *Manananggal*, etc. The *aswang* is a shape- shifting demon, humanlike by day but transforms into different monstrous forms at night. The *aswang* can change from a human to an animal form, usually as a bat, a pig or a black dog.*

^ Sering, Jose C.(1998).*Reminiscences: An Autobiography of Gov. Jose C. Sering.* Surigao City: Siargao Historical and Cultural Foundation.

* Clark, Jordan. (2017). *Creatures & Mythical Beings from Philippine Folklore & Mythology.* Retrieved from https://www.aswangproject.com/creatures-mythical-beings-philippine-folklore-mythology/

Swimming in Lambog Waterfalls, Christina Buo, 2013

In the forest of San Roque, a village situated eight kilometers from the town center of Pilar, we followed a nature trail, wading through shallow, rapid-flowing, cold streams, leaping from rock to rock, and clambering over the slippery ground and wild plants, until at last, we found Lambog Waterfalls. There it was, water falling effervescent and ever-clear down the surface of a rock, in the heart of the woods. We rushed towards it, falling water sending spray at our faces with gale force as we frolicked in the blast.

WISH UPON A FULL MOON

Night gives way to the Rising Moon,
casting magic and mystery over the lagoon.

General Luna, Siargao Island.
Painting by Christina Buo

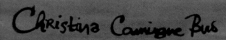

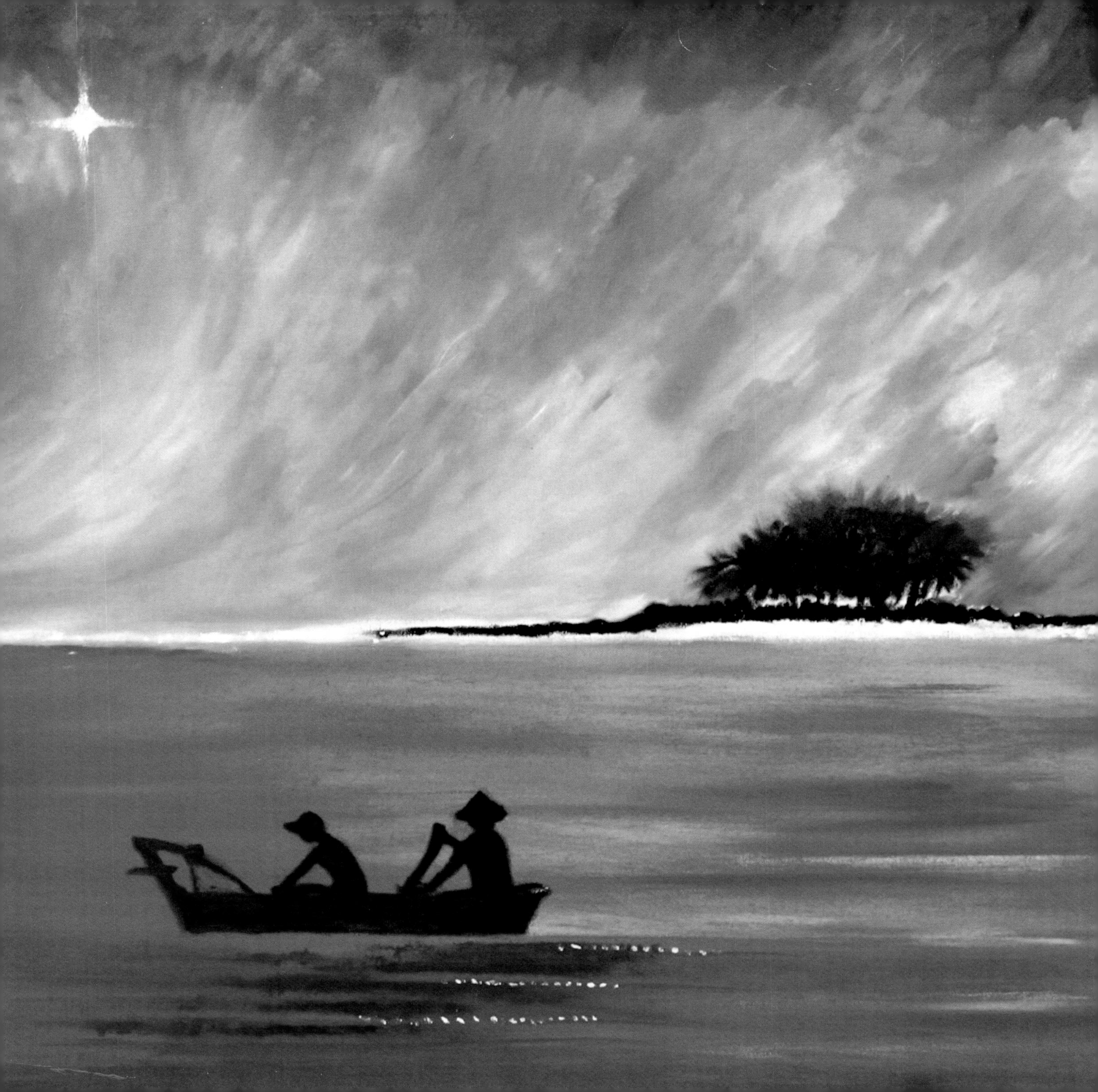